Vegetable Gardening for Beginners

Vegetable Gardening
for Beginners

A SIMPLE GUIDE TO GROWING
VEGETABLES AT HOME

Jill McSheehy

Illustrations by Enya Todd

ROCKRIDGE
PRESS

For general information on our other products and services or to obtain technical support, please contact our Customer Care Department within the United States at (866) 744-2665 or outside the United States at (510) 253-0500.

Interior and Cover Designer: Erin Yeung
Art Producer: Meg Baggott
Editor: Ada Fung and Claire Yee
Production Editor: Ruth Sakata Corley
Illustrations © 2020 Enya Todd

Author photo by Crystal Malloy Photography

ISBN: Print 978-1-64611-537-2 | eBook 978-1-64611-538-9
R0

In memory of my grandparents, Hobert and Ruth Alexander, the farmers I didn't get the chance to know. I have to wonder if they're smiling from heaven, watching their granddaughter tend her own plot of land.

Contents

Introduction

"Jill, would you go out to the garden and get me a green pepper?"

"Okaaaay . . ." I replied. "What does it look like?"

I don't recall this exchange, but my mom was quick to bring it up when I announced, as a 32-year-old, my new gardening venture.

I had just quit my job as Business Development Manager of a Ford dealership in order to stay home with my children, then aged six and two. To help ease the reduction of our household income, I figured growing some of our food would contribute in a different yet tangible way.

The problem? I had absolutely no idea how to get started or what to do. But I was determined, and I dove into every gardening resource I could find. I spent months combing through information. I kept a meticulous notebook on soil, crops, garden layouts, pests, and diseases.

But even the most basic gardening information—the kind that assumed absolutely no gardening knowledge—was still slightly beyond my reach. I ended up learning the way many gardeners do: by diving in and adjusting as I went.

My first garden yielded enough to hook me. As the years passed and I gained more knowledge and experience, I realized I wanted to share this passion with others, specifically, others with no prior knowledge of vegetable gardening. In January 2017 I launched the Beginner's Garden Podcast and began writing regular "how-to" articles on my blog, all for the beginning gardener I used to be.

While I'm grateful for the gardening books that got me started, what you hold in your hands is the book I wish I'd had.

In part 1, I'll teach you everything you need to know to get started with your own vegetable garden, beginning with some key decisions you need to make way before

PART ONE

A Step-by-Step Guide to Starting and Sustaining a Vegetable Garden

you purchase your first seeds. For example, what kind of garden do you want? Where will it go? How large? What tools do you need? What should you grow and when should you plant?

Then you'll learn about building and filling your garden beds or containers, starting seeds indoors, and transplanting. I'll discuss options for watering, mulching, and vertical gardening. Then, you'll learn how to harvest and store your bounty. Finally, I'll talk about what to do at the end of the growing season, because my hope is that this year is only the first of many wonderful gardening years for you.

Once you have the basics down, you can dive into part 2, where you'll learn about more than 30 common vegetables and herbs in the home garden and, of course, get the specifics on how to grow, harvest, and use them. I hope this section gets dog-eared and soil-stained from repeated use.

Are you ready to get started?

CHAPTER ONE

An Introduction to Vegetable Gardening

A successful vegetable garden begins with a solid understanding of basic gardening principles. You need to understand the "why" and the "what" before diving into the "how." Before you browse seed catalogs or pick up a shovel or even skip to the vegetable profiles, tempting as that might be, read this chapter carefully. This foundation will give you the knowledge to begin your vegetable gardening journey.

Why Grow Your Own Vegetables?

Backyard gardeners grow vegetables for many different reasons. Although I started with the goal of saving money, many gardeners begin for the simple joy a garden provides.

Any gardener will tell you that homegrown food tastes better. Science is also starting to confirm what gardeners have intuitively known for centuries: Home-grown food is more nutritious. Foods grown in rich, organic soils boast greater nutrient content and fewer toxic chemicals than their conventionally grown counterparts.

Studies also confirm not only the physical health benefits of gardening but the mental health aspects as well. Basically, after a few hours in the garden you'll feel better. How great is that?

Your reason for starting a garden may vary slightly from that of other gardeners, but just know this: Your first taste of a homegrown vegetable may change your life.

Why Organic?

Organic gardening is a long-term approach that yields beneficial diversity in terms of soil health, insects, and the garden ecosystem as a whole. But why is diversity important?

Diversity of soil microbes enables plants to access nutrients in the soil. Many of those microbes cannot survive in gardens that regularly receive synthetic fertilizer.

Diversity of beneficial insects keeps—with few exceptions—pest insect populations in check. Broad-spectrum insecticides kill both beneficial and pest insects.

Simply put, nonorganic gardening results in an unhealthy cycle of synthetic additions, which has negative local and global implications. Organic gardening builds the soil, the plants, and the garden ecosystem. Over time, organic gardeners find their gardens healthier, easier to maintain, and more productive.

7 Things to Know Before You Grow

Grow what you eat. Before the mouthwatering photos in seed catalogs lure you into trying a myriad of vegetables, pause for a moment. Make a list of the vegetables your family actually enjoys eating. Then, consider which of those you want to grow. The last thing you want is a bed full of kale when nobody in your family likes it. Focus on the vegetables your family wants to eat and learn to grow those well.

Don't be afraid to experiment. What if your family *might* like kale? Or what if you can't stop thinking about purple carrots or cute cucamelons? By all means, make room for them. Earmark a small section of your garden for experimental crops. I call them "rookies" because they're "trying out" for a permanent spot. But a garden of only experiments will probably disappoint. Keep most of your space for your family's favorites, and fit in a few rookies to keep it fun.

Be patient. Your local garden center may display tomato plants in February, but that doesn't mean you can plant them in your garden in the middle of winter. Nor does an early spring warm spell signal planting time. Seasoned gardeners have learned (through many overeager attempts) that waiting for the proper time to plant produces the best results. Fight temptation and follow the guidelines in chapter 2 and the plant profiles in part 2 to know when to plant. In most cases, this will require patience, but it will be worth it.

Understand that not everything will grow well in your climate. Every garden has different growing conditions that make some crops flourish and others struggle. Though the plant profiles in part 2 will guide you in a general sense, you will learn which plants work in your garden by trying them out.

Embrace failure. What if I told you that failure can be one of your greatest assets? No, I'm not talking about the total failure of your garden. I'm talking about small disappointments, which we all have. When you do fail, instead of giving in or giving up entirely, find the cause of the failure. From there, you can either adjust your garden for the current season or plan to change it for the next year. One of my greatest successes—learning to plant squash and zucchini at the end of the summer for a fall harvest—came after a devastating failure, when squash vine borers killed my midsummer planting. By expecting and embracing failure, you set yourself up for future success.

Mother Nature has the last word. We shouldn't use the weather as an excuse for every crop failure, but we do need to consider real weather conditions that affect our plants. Tomatoes struggle more with fungal issues in rainy springs, and summer crops provide bigger harvests when a fall frost comes late. Consider these factors before deciding whether to repeat a crop or try another one.

Take it easy and take it slow. Starting a small garden doesn't require a huge investment of money or time; a few starter tools will suffice. Nor do you need to spend hours in research. Get the basics down but protect yourself from information overload. As you gain experience, you'll have fun exploring more advanced techniques and ideas, but save that for later. For now, focus on what's really important and enjoy the process.

Common Gardening Terms

Annual plant: any vegetable or herb that starts and finishes its growth in one season, regardless of where it is grown. Examples: basil, lettuce, tomatoes.

Biennial plant: any nonfruiting vegetable or herb that, when grown under ideal conditions, produces seeds via a seed stalk in the second year of growth. Examples: carrots, onions, parsley.

Bolting: when a nonfruiting vegetable or herb sends up a seed stalk sooner than it should. Usually, bolting is caused by stressful weather conditions such as heat or drought. Examples: broccoli, cilantro, lettuce, onions.

Companion planting: growing different vegetables, herbs, or flowers beside each other for a favorable result such as pest control, disease prevention, or fitting more plants into the space.

Compost: a healthy, fertile, earthy mix produced from the breakdown of raw organic materials.

Container garden: a planting area where the soil is entirely "contained" within a pot or bed, and the plants' roots do not have access to the ground.

Cool-season crop: any vegetable or herb that prefers the cooler weather of spring or fall and does not grow well in the heat. Cool-season crops vary in their tolerance for cold or heat. Some tolerate very cold temperatures, but all cool-season crops will survive frosts.

Days to maturity: the average length of time it takes for a vegetable or herb to reach maturity and begin bearing a harvest. (If seeds are started indoors, days to maturity begin when plant is planted in the garden.)

Direct sow: planting a seed outdoors, directly in the ground, raised bed, or container.

Frost dates: the calendar dates on which your area typically experiences its last frost in spring and its first frost in fall. Keep in mind this is the *average*, so actual frost dates can vary within 2 weeks on either side of these dates. You can find your average frost dates by contacting your local extension service or searching online (see Resources, page 149).

Full sun: six to eight hours or more of direct, unfiltered sunlight per day. Many plants require full sun; some tolerate partial sun, which means 4 to 6 hours of sunlight.

Germination: when a seed begins its growth and sends a sprout above the soil surface and roots below the soil surface.

Growing zone or gardening zone: In the United States, growing zones correspond to the average minimum temperature a particular location experiences in the winter. Knowing your growing zone will help you understand which perennial crops will survive the winter.

Harvest category: in what time period and for how long a particular crop is expected to yield a harvest. In this book, harvest categories include the following: one harvest (crops will harvest all at once), quick burst (crops will yield a harvest for a period of 2 to 4 weeks), all season (crops will produce all season, usually until the first frost), and weather dependent (crops can be harvested until weather conditions cause the plant to bolt).

Mulch: a layer of organic material added to the top of the soil for the purpose of weed prevention, water retention, soil-temperature regulation, and erosion control. Examples: wood chips, fallen leaves, pine needles, grass clippings, organic hay or straw.

Organic matter: any addition to your garden that is or was living or produced by a living organism. Examples: leaves, wood chips, manure.

Perennial plant: any vegetable or herb that, by its nature, will continue to grow season after season if grown in the ideal growing zone. If it is grown in a zone colder than it can tolerate, it will grow like an annual plant and, unless protected, will die over the winter. Examples: peppers, rosemary, oregano.

Raised bed garden: any planting area that is "raised" above the ground, typically between 6 inches and 3 feet. Most have structural sides to contain the soil and an open bottom where the plants' roots can reach the native soil beneath.

Soil pH: the level of acidity or alkalinity of the soil, which enables plant uptake of the maximum amount of nutrients available. Most vegetables thrive in soil with a pH of 6.0 to 7.0.

Soil temperature: the temperature of the soil at the depth of about 1 inch. Different varieties of seeds require different soil temperatures in order to germinate.

Succession planting: planting crops at different times, sometimes one after another in the same space, to get staggered harvests or multiple harvests in one garden space. Related to succession planting, relay planting means planting a second crop near the first crop toward the end of the first crop's harvest date. They grow together for a period of time before the first crop gets pulled out.

Tilth: the physical condition of soil in regard to its structure and suitability for a plant to grow well in it. An ideal soil tilth possesses proper aeration and drainage while retaining optimum moisture.

Transplant: a baby plant that will be planted in the ground after having been started from seed indoors or purchased from a nursery. Transplanting is the act of planting a baby plant (seedling) into the ground.

Trellis: any structure that supports the vertical growth of a vegetable with a vining growth habit, such as pole beans or cucumbers.

Warm-season crop: any vegetable or herb that prefers warmer summer weather and will not survive a frost.

Best Gardens for Beginners

What do you envision when you think of a vegetable garden? Vegetables in neat, uniform rows in a dedicated plot of land? But an in-ground garden isn't necessarily the best option for a beginner.

In-ground gardens can be highly productive, but there are variables you can't always control the first year, such as soil quality and pH. You also might have to clear the new land, perhaps tilling it or covering the soil for several months prior to planting.

Issues such as these are why container gardening and raised beds are so popular. Let's explore your options.

Container Gardening

In a container garden, vegetables and herbs grow in a limited space, such as a pot or large planter. Many beginners enjoy container gardens because the labor involved is minimal. You don't have to prepare the ground, and weeding is almost nonexistent. You can also place your pots in the best location for the plants you're growing.

But container gardening isn't free of challenges. The cost of the containers and soil can add up. Plants in containers require great attention to watering, and in the heat of summer may need watering several times per day. Container plants also need more fertilization, because the continual watering leaches away nutrients and the plants cannot access nutrients in ground soil.

With proper attention and care, however, container gardens are rewarding. Great options for container growing include lettuce, greens, snap peas, peppers, tomatoes, and herbs.

Raised Bed Gardening

Raised beds combine the best features of in-ground and container gardens. Like containers, with proper mulching, you won't need to weed as often. But unlike containers, the plants' ability to send their roots into the native soil to access water and nutrients cuts down on both watering and fertilizing. Raised bed gardens, when done right, are very attractive. (Many people build raised beds on top of a solid surface such as paved ground. This design acts more like a container garden in terms of soil, water, fertilization, and drainage requirements.)

The biggest downside to raised beds is the initial cost and labor. You also cannot easily move them if you change your mind about the ideal location. Predesigned kits available at garden centers make the labor barrier easier to overcome.

Most gardeners who choose raised beds find the trade-offs to be worth it both in time saved over the season and their overall gardening experience. Almost all crops grow well in raised beds; some popular ones include tomatoes, beans, broccoli, peppers, onions, and zucchini.

Vertical Gardening

Whether you choose an in-ground garden, a container garden, a raised bed garden, or a combination of all three, consider adding vertical gardening to your plan.

When you train vining plants on a trellis, you make space for more crops in the container or bed. Plus, the better airflow achieved with vertical gardening reduces the risk of many common plant diseases.

Exercise your creative side: You can use free materials such as gathered sticks to build a trellis or make a small investment in a cattle-panel arch trellis. Sturdy trellises can last for many seasons. We explore several options in chapter 3.

Great crops for vertical gardening include pole beans, climbing peas, cucumbers, and even melons.

Growing in the Ground

Maybe you don't have the budget for containers or raised beds. Or maybe you've always wanted a traditional in-ground garden, and you're determined to make it happen. Here are five qualities to look for when choosing to grow your garden directly in the ground.

Soil pH and balanced nutrients. The health of your garden soil will directly correspond to the health and productivity of your plants. I recommend getting your soil tested at a professional lab. Most counties offer this service through their cooperative extension locations for free or a small fee. From there, you will know what amendments you need to add to the soil, if any.

Loamy soil mixture. Soil is made up of sand, silt, clay, or a combination of them. The ideal garden soil is loamy, meaning it has a balanced mixture of these components. If your soil leans heavily toward one element, your yields will not be as great. A professional soil test will tell you what soil type you have, and you can always amend a less-than-loamy soil with organic matter such as compost. But do note that it can take years to see a big difference.

Well-draining area. Plants will not thrive in standing water, so unless your soil contains a high amount of sand, you'll want to place your in-ground garden in an area that is slightly elevated or at least not lower than the surrounding land.

Slight slope. Ideal in-ground gardens have an almost undetectable slope. This means the land will drain well, but its gentle angle will also prevent nutritious topsoil and protective mulch from washing away during heavy rainfalls.

Away from trees. Trees inhibit growth in two ways. First, roots that extend under a garden steal water and nutrients. Second, trees shade the garden, which is not ideal for plants that need full sun.

Essential Gardening Tools

We cover specific materials needed for each type of garden in chapter 3, but here are the must-have tools for any garden type.

For Indoor Seed Starting

For starting seeds indoors, this is what you'll need:

Seed-starting containers. We discuss specific options in chapter 4, but the most common container is a seed-starting tray. Trays with six cells make transplanting easier, plus you can customize the number of trays based on how many plants you plan to grow indoors.

Seed-starting mix. Seeds require what is called a "soilless mix" to reduce disease in young seedlings. Although you can make your own, small bags of seed-starting mix can be purchased at most garden supply stores or online.

Grow light. The light from a window is usually not enough to get your seedlings off to the healthiest start. Invest in a grow light. Many beginning gardeners find a 2-foot T5 fluorescent light sufficient, but you should consider LED options. LED technology continues to improve, and the bulbs are becoming more affordable. The biggest consideration is how far the light extends; you want to make sure all the seedlings you start will be covered in light.

For Starting and Sustaining Your Garden

You'll find that the right garden tool makes a world of difference. These are my favorites:

Garden gloves. Garden gloves do more than keep dirt off your skin. Nitrile gloves that contour to your hands give you a better grip when hoeing and weeding, dexterity when planting, and protection from hidden thorns or stickers.

Rain gauge. A simple rain gauge found at any garden center will help you know when you need to supplement your plants with water.

Shovel and hoe. These tools are must-haves for adding and incorporating soil, mulch, and other amendments. A hoe will also help with planting seeds in rows and with heavy-duty weeding. Choose a design with a stainless steel head; a rubber grip is also a plus.

Soil thermometer. Planting when the weather is warm but the soil is still cool results in lowered rates of germination, rotting seeds, and stunted plants. A soil thermometer will help you know when to plant your seeds. Choose a quick-read digital thermometer for ease of use. You will find the optimum soil temperature for each plant in the plant profiles in part 2.

Trowel. The primary function of a trowel is to help you easily transplant seedlings or plants. But you will also use it to add compost, fill containers, and harvest root crops. A stainless steel trowel with a rubber grip makes this multifunction tool comfortable and durable.

Watering can. A watering can is essential for container gardens. And though raised beds and in-ground gardens often require more than hand-watering, all gardeners need a watering can during transplanting and for adding diluted liquid fertilizer when needed. Choose a two-gallon can with a removable sprinkle nozzle. Use the sprinkle nozzle when watering seeds and seedlings, and remove the nozzle for more thorough watering of established plants.

For Harvesting and Storing Vegetables

Thinking about harvesting and storing vegetables when planning a garden may seem like jumping the gun, but when harest time arrives, you will be glad you prepared.

Bucket or basket. A bucket or basket is great to have handy while you pick. If you choose a basket, one with a tighter weave is preferable in order to prevent smaller vegetables (such as green beans) from slipping through.

Garden knife. Some vegetables (e.g., zucchini, cabbage, and broccoli) are easier to harvest with a knife rather than pruning shears. A garden knife makes a clean cut without damaging the plant.

Pruning shears. You can easily harvest many vegetables and herbs by hand, whereas others (e.g., peppers, okra, and cucumbers) require a precise cut to prevent damaging the remaining plant. A pair of pruning shears is a multifunction tool that is my go-to for harvesting.

Reusable produce bags. Once you harvest your crops, most of them (with the exception of tomatoes and a few others) require prompt refrigeration. Choose resealable zip-top bags to last you season after season.

10 Steps to Successful Vegetable Gardening

Select the type of garden that best suits your lifestyle. Will you grow your vegetables in the ground, a raised bed, containers, or a combination of all three? Whichever you choose, you want to ensure you can afford it both financially and in terms of time and physical demands. An in-ground garden requires less up-front cost, though it may demand more time and labor. Raised beds and container gardens require cost in materials and labor, but the trade-off of free time over the course of the season makes them worth considering.

Choose the garden's location with care. Where you plant your garden will directly impact its success. A thriving garden, for example, has ample sunlight and access to water. And the closer the garden can be to your home, the more likely it is that you will walk in your garden daily—another key to success.

Know your zone and frost dates and understand the difference. Your garden zone helps you understand your general climate, but more precisely it tells you which plants should survive your winter. A common misconception is that garden zones indicate *when* to plant, but that's not the case. Your average last-frost date in spring and first-frost date in fall dictate when to plant each vegetable. You can find resources to help you identify your zone and frost dates on page 149.

Keep records. We think we will remember every detail of our gardens, but we don't. By keeping records of planting dates, garden layout, pest issues, and other variables,

Other Nice-to-Have Tools

All gardeners find some tools well worth the investment, even if they are not absolutely necessary. If you have the budget, consider investing in these handy favorites.

Drip irrigation or soaker hose(s) with timer. Gardens in almost every climate will require supplemental irrigation at some point. When coupled with an automatic timer, drip irrigation lines or soaker hoses save you time to do other garden tasks.

Micro-tip pruning shears. Micro-tip pruning shears make quick work of more delicate tasks, such as harvesting tomatoes, small peppers, and herbs. Though an all-purpose pruner is enough, I find having both to be helpful.

Moisture meter. A plant responds to overwatering and underwatering in the same way. A moisture meter instantly tells you whether you need to water your plant or bed. Although helpful in all gardens, this meter is most useful for container gardeners.

Stool or kneeling pad. From planting to weeding to harvesting, your back and knees will thank you when you can comfortably sit or kneel to work. My favorite garden seat is a folding stool with pockets for tools.

Three-pronged fork. For loosening soil ahead of planting or for smaller weeding jobs, a three-pronged fork makes the task easier. Choose a stainless steel option with fine tips and a rubber grip.

Wheelbarrow. Transporting soil, compost, and mulch is part of any gardener's life. A wheelbarrow makes these tasks infinitely easier.

you can make adjustments each season. This will come in handy with future crop rotation, plant variety selection, pest control, and more.

Start small. A common mistake beginning gardeners make is planting too much. As the season progresses, they find they can't keep up with maintaining the garden, which leads to discouragement and burnout. It's best to start with a few plants in a smaller space; you can always expand in the future. The goal at the end of the season is for you to want more next year, and this happens when gardeners are conservative in the scope of their first gardens.

Learn the basic conditions in which the vegetables you want to grow will thrive. Most vegetables loosely fit into the category of "cool-season crop" or "warm-season crop." Knowing which of your favorite vegetables fit into each category will help you understand when to plant, based on your climate (zone). This also helps you make the most of your space through succession planting, which we discuss in chapter 2. The plant profiles in part 2 will help you understand these differences, as well as give you general planting dates.

Prioritize soil health. In an organic garden, soil health directly corresponds to plant health and harvest. Healthy plants not only yield greater harvests, but they also better resist disease and pest pressure. Start with high-quality soil and plan to regularly add organic material, such as compost, worm castings, and mulch.

Know the mature size of each vegetable before you plant. A common regret of new gardeners is their lack of attention to proper plant spacing. Spacing directly impacts the health and productivity of plants. If plants grow too close together, they'll compete for nutrients, the overall harvest will be smaller, and disease and pests will be more of a problem. Conversely, if plants are too far apart, weeds will take over, stealing nutrients and water. By knowing the mature size of each vegetable before planting a seed or transplant, you can set up the healthiest environment for your plants from the beginning.

Plan for irrigation and mulch. Situate your garden close to a water source, and then consider how you want to irrigate when rainwater falls short. Do you want to hand-water, or would you prefer a drip system or soaker hose? Make these decisions before you plant. Also, plan to add organic mulch, such as wood chips or shredded fall leaves, after your plants are established. Mulch regulates water, reduces evaporation, prevents weeds, and enriches the soil.

Prepare your mind-set. Beginning gardeners have high expectations, which is completely normal. But every garden has its successes and failures. (Even the most experienced gardeners will tell you this.) Learning from both failures and successes sets you up for long-term productivity as a home vegetable gardener.

CHAPTER TWO

Planning Your Vegetable Garden

Are you itching to start? I'm excited for you, too, but before you begin gathering tools or ordering seeds, you need a plan. The difference between a successful, thriving garden and one that doesn't produce well is often found in garden planning.

In this chapter, we'll talk about important considerations such as where to plant, when to plant, what to plant, and how to successfully grow in your climate.

Where Should You Put Your Garden?

The first decision you need to make is where to place your garden. Because it's difficult to change the location of your garden once you've built it, you should consider the following factors carefully.

Follow the Sun

Many of the most popular vegetables in home gardens require full sun. "Full sun" means a minimum of six to eight hours of unshaded, unfiltered sunlight during the growing season. Even though some vegetables and herbs tolerate less sunlight, it's best to choose the sunniest location possible for your garden.

Note that the angle of the sun's track changes throughout the year, so the sunniest spot in the off-season won't be the same as during the growing season. Consider where the sun will track in the height of summer. Also, keep in mind that a location near a deciduous tree may receive full sun in the winter but will remain mostly shaded in the summer when the leaves return.

Notice where a potential garden space would lie in relation to structures such as your home or a shed. In all but the hottest climates, gardens facing west and south will benefit the most from ample afternoon sun.

Certain plants prefer some shade, especially if you live in a hot climate. You can always plant taller vegetables around shade-loving plants, but you can't change the shade cast from structures or trees.

Site It Within Sight

"Out of sight, out of mind." It may not seem like it now, but in the middle of the growing season, gardens not within easy walking distance of the house suffer more neglect than gardens located close by.

There is a saying that "the best fertilizer is a gardener's shadow." Daily walks in the garden allow you to spot and treat small issues before they become big problems. Catching problems early will lead to a healthier, more successful garden.

Access to Water (But Not Too Much)

If possible, try to position your garden near a water source such as an outdoor spigot. Easy access to supplemental irrigation will help you stay on top of the watering needs of your plants.

However, too much water can be a bad thing. Avoid placing your garden near rain gutters or in low-lying areas. I unknowingly situated my first garden, an entirely in-ground garden, in the lowest area of my property. Winter and spring rains puddled, and few plants survived. Take note of natural slopes in your land, and avoid placing your garden in the lowest-lying areas.

Making the Best of What You Have

Unless you have a large property with multiple site choices, you may only have one or, at best, a few options for your garden's location. Perhaps your yard has more shade than you'd prefer, or you wish you had more space. Maybe the only sunny spot happens to be the lowest-lying area of your yard. If finding the optimum location seems impossible, consider these work-arounds.

No getting around the shade?

- Plant vegetables and herbs that tolerate shade. Vegetables that produce fruit, such as tomatoes and cucumbers, require full sun. However, leafy plants (e.g., lettuce) and most root crops (e.g., beets and carrots) grow well in partial shade.
- If the shade comes from trees, consider trimming some lower branches to allow more light through.
- When a structure casts unwanted shade, add reflective material to the wall or paint it a light color. The reflection increases the amount of light that gets to the plants.
- If you're going to grow vegetables in containers, place the containers on rollers, and move fruiting plants into the sunlight throughout the day.

CONTINUED

Small space?

- Plant compact, highly productive plants. Excellent choices include squash, cucumbers, peppers, and determinate tomatoes (see tomato profile, page 126, for definition).
- Add vertical gardening to create room for more crops. Carrots grow well under pole beans; lettuce can be grown under vining cucumbers.
- Use companion planting to place crops with a higher canopy (e.g., tomatoes and peppers) next to those with lower growth habits (e.g., lettuce and beets).

No well-draining area?

If your entire property sits in water during rainy seasons, raised beds can be the perfect gardening solution. Aim for the raised bed to be at a height of at least 10 inches. That way, the soil can drain well without soaking up too much excess water from the ground below.

Still no ideal location?

Consider growing your vegetables at a local community garden or allotment. Ask around to find out about your options.

What Type of Garden Should You Have?

Now that you've found the best location for your garden, it's time to think about which gardening method you will use.

Raised Bed or Container?

Most raised garden beds have no solid base and therefore are open to the ground, allowing plant roots access to the soil below, whereas a container plant grows in a confined space.

Raised beds require simple construction, whereas containers can easily be purchased ready to go. Both types need to be filled with soil, but if you have access to native ground soil, you can use a mixture of that in a raised bed, saving money on soil costs.

Containers demand more frequent watering, which is a consideration if you're often away from home. Raised beds allow more growing options, but typically container gardens require less maintenance and labor overall.

Figuring Out Size and Shape

Most gardeners who can give an hour per week to garden tasks during peak season can easily manage a few raised beds. Although raised beds come in a variety of shapes and sizes, I recommend sticking with a conventional size. A simple 4-by-8-foot, 4-by-12-foot, or 3-by-6-foot bed provides plenty of plant layout options.

If you choose container gardening, you will likely find your limits not in the amount of time you can give but rather in your budget. Purchasing containers and soil can become costly. You can always start with a few containers and add more as your budget allows.

Mix and Match Garden Types

What if you can't decide on the type of garden you want? Many gardeners enjoy growing with a mixture of these forms. I grow vegetables and herbs in the ground, in raised beds, and in containers. Because there are pros and cons to each method, I use each to my advantage.

Frequently harvested plants such as herbs and greens are ideal container plants. Some vegetables, such as onions and peppers, thrive in the warm, well-draining (but not too well-draining) soil of raised beds. And some crops, such as corn, are best suited to the larger space of an in-ground garden.

Regardless of the place, remember vertical gardening. Tomatoes, cucumbers, and pole beans, for example, benefit from trellising whether in containers, raised beds, or the ground.

What Should You Grow?

Besides growing what you enjoy eating, other factors such as where you live and the gardening method you've chosen will also help determine what you grow. Let's take a look at these considerations.

Determine Your Growing Zone

Knowing your growing zone will help you understand your general growing climate and which plants will likely thrive there. Divided into 11 categories, growing zones are calculated based on the average annual minimum temperature in each location. (See the map on page 148 to find your zone.)

Growing zones were created to help gardeners understand which *perennial* plants will survive the winter in a particular location. Because annual plants complete their life cycle in one season and do not survive the winter, growing zones technically do not apply to them.

Although your zone won't matter for most vegetables and herbs you grow, knowing it can help you understand which plants grow best in certain seasons, which plant varieties may grow better, and which plants may not grow at all.

For example, gardeners in the cooler zones 1 to 4 might grow cool-weather crops all summer, but their season isn't long enough to support heat-loving crops such as okra and large melons. Gardeners in warmer zones 7 to 11 usually can't grow cool-weather crops such as lettuce in the summer, but they can grow them in fall and winter.

Seed packets, seed catalogs, and plant tags are great resources. They specify if a plant can grow in your zone. We talk more about this in chapter 3.

Identifying Microclimates

In addition to knowing your growing zone, it's important to consider factors unique to your yard. The nuances of your specific location, or *microclimate*, alter your growing conditions and can also affect when you get frosts. Frost dates are key to knowing when and what to plant (see page 14).

Microclimates can occur around structures, mountains, bodies of water, slopes, and more. Gardens planted next to a south-facing wall, for example, may have higher heat that prevents tomato fruit from forming in warmer zones, but creates a greater yield of peppers in cooler zones.

Gardens in the shadow of a mountain, in a valley, or at the bottom of a slope may get frosts later in the spring and earlier in the fall than surrounding higher elevations. This type of microclimate may require a gardener to delay summer planting or to cover frost-prone plants.

These are just a few examples of microclimate variations, and you should pay attention to how your plants respond to your microclimate. Make note of your area's average last- and first-frost dates and compare them to what you actually experience from year to year. If your conditions vary from what is considered average for your area, you can adjust your crops and the timing of your plantings accordingly.

Consider Your Garden Type and Space

Most plants are happy to grow in containers, raised beds, or the ground. However, some are better suited to one form or another.

Some herbs (e.g., mint, lemon balm, and oregano) spread aggressively, which makes them ideal for a container. If you plant them in a raised or in-ground bed, they will take over and smother other plants.

Some crops are considered "heavy feeders," which means they need more nutrients than others. Therefore, although heavy feeders such as tomatoes, squash, cabbage, and broccoli grow well in containers, they enjoy the moisture-holding capacity of raised beds, and the greater access to soil nutrients reduces the need for regular supplemental fertilizer. Raised beds are also ideal for crops that require more plants for a plentiful harvest, such as beans, peas, and okra.

Some plants also need more space than others. If you're looking to maximize the yield of your garden, a container full of greens that can feed you for months may be a better choice than a container with one cabbage plant that will give you one head.

Pick Plants That Get Along

Vegetables and herbs benefit from companion planting. Scientific research on the topic remains scarce, but we do know that the more diverse your vegetables, herbs, and flowers are, the healthier your garden will be. Some plants do seem to offer a measure of pest control to nearby plants. For example, icicle radishes may repel squash bugs and cucumber beetles.

Conversely, some plants negatively affect others when planted in close proximity. Broccoli and tomatoes, for example, both uptake high levels of calcium. Planting them together could result in smaller broccoli heads and blossom-end rot in tomatoes. Also beware that plants in the same families (e.g., cabbage and cauliflower) often are visited by the same pests, are afflicted by the same diseases, and take up similar nutrients from the soil. (Plants that share similar characteristics, such as appearance, general growth habits, and seed and seedling presentation, are grouped into plant families.)

In addition to pest control and nutrient needs, there are other benefits to companion planting. Vegetables with varying growth habits and nutrient needs benefit each other (such as planting cooler-weather crops in the shade of heat-loving ones). This is also an excellent way to maximize a small space.

Although some companion planting combinations may benefit your garden, don't dive too deeply into it now. Start with these suggestions and experiment with other combinations later.

Common Companion Planting Combinations

PLANT	FRIENDS	FOES	REASON
Tomatoes	Basil Carrots	Potatoes Corn	Carrots attract ladybugs, whose larvae feed on aphids. Basil is thought to repel aphids, hornworm, thrips, and armyworms. Potatoes and tomatoes are both susceptible to fungal diseases, and tomatoes and corn both attract the corn earworm and tomato fruitworm.
Squash/ Zucchini	Marigold Nasturtium Thyme Icicle Radishes		The herbs and radish may reduce populations of squash bugs and cucumber beetles.
Peas	Carrots Radishes	Beans	Shallow-rooted peas pair nicely with root crops. Peas and beans have similar nutrient needs and grow best apart.

PLANT	FRIENDS	FOES	REASON
Spinach Lettuce Greens	Peppers		As the summer heats up, the cool-weather crops benefit from the shade of the growing pepper plants.
Carrots	Onions Radishes	Dill	Onions repel the carrot rust fly. Radishes grow quickly while carrots grow slowly. Radishes can be harvested to make room for carrots, maximizing the output of the space. Dill is said to inhibit the growth of carrots.
Cabbage	Thyme Nasturtium Marigold Onions	Broccoli Kale	Herbs and onions repel cabbage worms, cabbage loopers, and caterpillars. Broccoli and kale both attract cabbage worms.
Cucumber	Beans Broccoli Lettuce Onions Peas Radishes	Squash/zucchini	Bush beans and other smaller vegetables grow at the base of a vining cucumber plant. Squash and zucchini share disease vulnerabilities with cucumbers, so it's best to separate them.

When and How Should You Plant Your Vegetables?

In this section, you're going to discover how to plan the timing of your plantings, start seeds indoors, plant directly in the garden, properly space your vegetables, and plan for crop rotation.

Figure Out Your Frost Date

Perhaps even more important than your garden zone, your average last- and first-frost dates are crucial to your planting decisions.

In the spring, you plant each crop a specified number of weeks before or after your average last-frost date, depending on the plant. The same goes for crops you plant for a fall harvest, relative to your average first-frost date in the fall.

You can find these dates by calling your local cooperative extension service or by visiting a website that will tell you your frost dates by zip code (see Resources, page 149). Remember, these dates are averages, which means frost can occur within 2 weeks on either side of these dates for any given year. In addition, your microclimate (see page 24) may affect these average frost dates.

Starting Seeds vs. Sowing Directly

Many first-time gardeners choose to plant only transplants from the local nursery or garden center. But for others, the idea of planting seeds excites them, not to mention that many plants (beans, for example) do not transplant well and are best planted from seed. In addition, seeds are comparatively inexpensive.

If you do choose to plant seeds, you need to decide whether to start seeds indoors or direct sow them into the garden.

Tomatoes and peppers are the most obvious choices to start from seed indoors. Their long growing time requires an earlier start in most seasons, and because they don't grow well in cool conditions, a controlled indoor environment is best. If you don't want to start these seeds indoors, purchasing transplants is recommended.

Other plants are best suited for direct sowing. Beans, squash, zucchini, peas, corn, carrots, spinach, and beets prefer being grown from seeds planted directly in the garden. Soil temperature is key for proper germination, and I strongly recommend purchasing an inexpensive soil thermometer to ensure the soil is warm enough for sowing.

Each plant you plan to grow will require different planting times and soil temperatures; refer to the plant profiles in part 2 for specifics. If you're pressed for time and want to ease into your first garden, feel free to skip starting your seeds indoors. Many beginning gardeners purchase young plants and transplant them. In addition, some vegetable seeds germinate and grow better when planted directly into the ground.

Spacing

How do you figure out how far apart to space seeds or transplants?

Proper spacing is important. If vegetables grow too close together, they compete for nutrients and water, reducing total yield. On the other hand, if they grow too far apart, weeds fill the vacant space.

Seed packets, plant tags, and the plant profiles in part 2 will give you direction on proper plant spacing. Seed packets generally direct you to "overseed," which means planting more seeds than will ultimately grow. After the seeds germinate, you remove extra seedlings by cutting them at soil level, in order to arrive at the final spacing. When using the profiles in this book as a guide, I recommend planting twice as many seeds and removing every other sprout if they all germinate.

Bear in mind that the recommended spacing on seed packets refers to rows of plants in a traditional in-ground garden. There are no pathways in containers and raised beds, so you won't need to leave as much room between rows. Instead, use the plant spacing recommendations for seeding, and plant in all directions. For example, you may be advised to plant bush bean seeds 3 inches apart in rows 2 feet apart, thinning after germination to a final spacing of 6 inches apart. In a raised bed or container, you can plant the seeds 3 inches apart in all directions, then thin to half the number of beans planted.

Of course, plant spacing guidelines are general guidelines. Try to get close, but don't worry about taking a ruler to the garden . . . unless you really want to.

Succession Planting

You can get twice the harvest from the same space by succession planting, which means planting a second crop after production ends from a first crop. An example of this is planting summer squash after you harvest and pull up bush beans.

Relay planting offers even more options. In relay planting, you plant a second crop next to a crop that is nearing its end of production. The two crops grow side by side until the first crop comes out. I use relay planting when I place bell pepper seedlings between mature spinach or lettuce plants. As the summer heats up, these cool-weather leafy plants bolt. I pull them up and the bell peppers take over.

To get the most out of succession planting, it helps to know whether a crop harvests all at once, all season long, or until heat or cold stops its production. Root crops harvest all at once and fall into the "one harvest" category, whereas bush beans and peas harvest over only a couple of weeks and fall into the "quick burst" category. Pole beans provide an "all season" harvest, producing until frost, and many greens are "weather dependent," meaning they keep producing until heat makes them bolt. Harvest categories for each vegetable are listed in part 2.

Here are some examples of harvest categories in relation to succession planting: Bush beans and determinate tomatoes, such as Roma, are quick-burst crops; you pick them over the course of a few weeks and then they're done. Once you pull these plants out, you can plant another round of the same crop or something else, perhaps summer squash or an early fall crop. On the other hand, pole beans and indeterminate tomatoes (most slicing tomatoes) produce all season, so you would not plan a succession crop for them.

As long as you follow the plant's natural preference for growing conditions and have a basic understanding of each plant's harvest period, the combinations for succession and relay planting are as plentiful as your imagination.

Crop Rotation

When you consider all the possible combinations of plant locations and then factor in having to rotate your crops from year to year, you may find your head spinning!

Thankfully, crop rotation isn't terribly complicated. Follow this basic formula: Avoid planting vegetables from the same plant family in the same place season after season. The reason for this is twofold. First, some diseases and pests that plague one family of plants persist in the soil. By rotating susceptible crops out of that area, you disrupt the disease and pest cycle. Second, different crops absorb different amounts of nutrients, and some actually contribute nutrients to the soil. For example, corn and squash require large amounts of nitrogen relative to other crops, so changing their location each season prevents depletion of the soil and stunted plants. Beans, on the other hand, add nitrogen to the soil, so your garden will benefit if you change their position each season so they can spread their love.

In the plant profiles in part 2, you will find each plant's family. This will help you when planning your beds or containers. If you decide to incorporate companion planting and succession planting, it may get a little more complicated, but don't sweat it. Just do your best to rotate as much as you can.

Full-Season Garden Plan

LOCATION	JAN	FEB	MAR	APR	MAY	JUN	JUL	AUG	SEP	OCT	NOV	DEC
Raised Bed 1			— Peas —			— Sweet Potatoes —						
Raised Bed 2			— Peas —			— Melons/Okra —						
Raised Bed 3			— Arugula/ Carrots/ Radishes —			— Zucchini —						Garlic
Container 1	— Garlic/Spinach —				— Peppers —							
Raised Bed 4			— Broccoli —			— Corn —			— Cabbage —			
Container 2			Onions/ Lettuce		— Peppers —							
Raised Bed 5			— Potatoes —			— Okra —						
Raised Bed 6			— Potatoes —			— Black-Eyed Peas —						
Raised Bed 7				— Roma Tomatoes —				Buck-wheat	— Broccoli —			
Arch Trellis 1				— Cucumbers —								
Raised Bed 8				— Indeterminate Tomatoes —								

QUICK-BURST HARVEST	ALL-SEASON HARVEST	HEAT-DEPENDENT	ONE HARVEST
Roma Tomatoes	Indeterminate Tomatoes	Peas	Sweet Potatoes
Corn	Pole Beans	Arugula	Potatoes
Bush Beans	Zucchini	Spinach	Carrots/Radishes
	Melons	Lettuce	Garlic
	Okra		Cabbage
	Peppers		Onions
	Cucumbers		

For each bed or space, sketch out each crop and how long it will remain in the ground based on its average days to maturity plus harvest time. Then fill in blank spaces with succession plantings for a full-season garden harvest.

Tip: Draw vertical lines at your average last and first frost dates to determine planting times.

Keeping a Gardening Journal

One of the most important things you can do to improve your garden year after year is to keep a gardening journal. It can be as simple or as elaborate as you want, but the key is to do it.

Record which plants you are growing, when you planted them, when you harvested, and any problems you encountered. Also, note any specific challenges such as pests or abnormal weather, for example, early heat, late frost, above-average rain, or departure from normal temperatures. When you plan for the following season, you can use this information to adjust your planting dates or other actions.

Be sure to map your garden layout in some way. Ideally, you will draw a garden layout ahead of planting, but I never fail to change something as I'm planting. You may think you'll remember where everything grew, but as the years go by, the seasons will start to run together in your mind. Keeping track of different layouts will help when you're planning crop rotations, and you'll be able to reference which companion planting and succession planting combinations worked and which didn't.

Keep track of harvests as well. Did you get more zucchini than you could eat? Maybe next season you should reduce the number of plants. Did you wish you had more tomatoes for canning? Next season you might earmark space for more.

Whether you purchase a journal designed for gardening, make notes in a spiral notebook, or use a phone app, keeping track of your garden will help you improve it in seasons to come.

SAMPLE GARDENING JOURNAL ENTRIES

CROP	DATE PLANTED IN GARDEN	DATE HARVEST BEGAN	DATE HARVEST ENDED	NOTES/PROBLEMS
Summer squash and zucchini	4/8	5/31	7/4	Harvested enough to eat fresh and freeze 6 bags of shredded zucchini. Had to pull plants due to powdery mildew and squash bugs.
Radishes	2/27	4/8	5/8	Planted with carrots; these were harvested before carrots needed the room; excellent companion plant.
Lettuce	3/6	4/19	6/9	Mix of Parris Island Cos and red romaine. Highly productive and didn't get bitter as early when the heat arrived in May.
Roma tomatoes	4/8	7/1	7/25	Early blight affected this year's crop more than normal.
Shelling peas	3/1	5/18	6/4	First time trying Lincoln peas. Didn't need a trellis; highly productive.
Onions	3/18	6/6	6/6	Planted late due to cold and rainy spring. Bulbs smaller size than usual.

Putting Your Plan into Motion

Knowledge is power, and now that you understand the concepts of deciding what to plant and where to plant it, you can finally pick up pencil and paper and start planning your vegetable garden. When compiling your plan, don't forget to use the plant profiles in part 2 for additional information. For any crops not listed in part 2, refer to seed packet instructions or an online resource. Here's a step-by-step guide:

1. List the crops you want to grow. Divide this list into two categories: must-grow and would like to grow.

2. Divide these crops into two sections: cool-season crops and warm-season crops.

3. For each plant, decide whether you want to start seeds indoors, purchase transplants, or direct sow.

4. Based on your decisions, write down the planting date for each crop. To do this, first find your average last-frost date and use the plant timing instructions.

5. Note the harvest category of each crop. Place a star beside any plants with a quick-burst or weather-dependent harvest; they are prime candidates for succession planting.

6. For each plant, look up the recommended plant spacing. Then decide how many plants (or how many rows) you will plant for each crop.

7. List any companion planting combinations you want to incorporate.

8. Brainstorm any vertical gardening ideas you want to try (see page 10).

9. For raised or in-ground beds, draw a layout grid of your garden space (graph paper is a great help). Each square represents 1 foot. If you're growing in containers, sketch out a top view of each container. If the container is circular, draw a square inside, noting the distance between the sides of the square.

10. In your layout, use a pencil to sketch in your must-grow crops. Then fill any remaining space with the crops you would like to grow. For the crops

with a star, decide how you will use succession planting in those spaces. Some areas may have two crops listed, if you plan to plant a second crop after the harvest of the first one.

11. Now that your garden layout is taking shape, adjust it as necessary. You may decide to add more containers or change the quantities of crops.

With your rough plan in place (don't worry, you can still change it!), it's time to start building your garden.

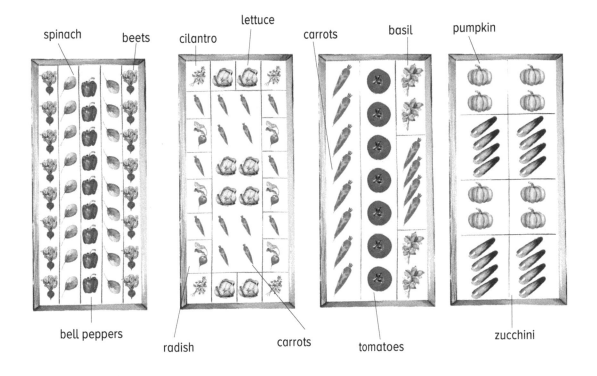

Using the spacing guidelines in the plant profiles, sketch a layout for each garden space. Tip: Use a pencil, so you can adjust plant placements as you plant. Sketching a layout ahead of time also helps you determine the quantity of seeds or plants you need to purchase.

CHAPTER THREE

Building Your Vegetable Garden

The concept of building or setting up your vegetable garden might seem a bit intimidating, but it doesn't have to be. Although gardeners love exercising creativity in building raised beds and containers, when you're first beginning, the most basic plans are usually the best. This chapter provides step-by-step instructions for creating a container garden, building a raised bed garden, adding vertical supports, and making an ideal soil mix.

How to Create a Container Garden

A container garden can be as simple or as complex as you wish. Once you learn how to choose your materials, what tools you need, and how to prepare your containers, you can get started.

Materials and Tools Needed

- Containers or pots
- Drill (if pot doesn't contain drainage holes)
- Potting soil
- Trowel

Containers come in all shapes, sizes, and materials. You can purchase containers, repurpose old gardening pots, use 5-gallon buckets, or invest in lightweight grow bags.

The size and depth of the container you use will depend on what plants you grow in them. Shallow-rooted plants (e.g., lettuce and greens) can grow in a space as little as 6 inches deep, but larger vegetables (e.g., tomatoes) require larger, deeper containers such as a 5- or 10-gallon pot.

Preparing and Modifying Containers

Getting your container ready for planting can mean simply selecting the pot and filling it with soil. However, there are other steps you should take to ensure you get the healthiest vegetables and have a positive experience.

1. Select your containers based on the vegetables you intend to plant. Take note of plant spacing and mature plant size to determine if multiple vegetables or herbs can grow in one pot.

2. If you're reusing gardening pots, wash them with a 10 percent bleach mixture to kill any pathogens remaining from a previous crop.

3. Unless you're using grow bags, ensure the pot contains several drainage holes. If the pot doesn't have holes, drill several holes in the bottom. Beware of containers with self-contained drainage trays. During heavy

rains, the water can fill the reservoir, and without the ability to drain, the saturated soil can kill your plants.

4. For containers deeper than 18 inches, you can place a smaller inverted pot in the bottom. This saves money (you use less soil) and reduces the weight.

5. Consider placing large containers on wheeled plant caddies, in case you ever need to change their location.

Filling Your Containers

For vegetables growing in containers, you need potting soil or potting mix. Garden soil (from your yard or in bags) should not be used because of its water-holding capacity and inability to drain well.

You can purchase bagged potting mix or mix your own (see page 45). If you choose a bagged mix, keep in mind that many nonorganic mixes contain synthetic fertilizer. If you choose an organic potting soil, you can add a granular, slow-release fertilizer, following the dosage instructions on the bag.

When you're ready to fill your container, leave only 1 to 2 inches of space at the top. The soil will compact, giving you more space for watering and mulch as the season progresses.

Growing Up: Stakes, Cages, Trellises, and More

Vegetables that climb, vine, or sprawl need some type of vertical support. The most commonly grown vegetables requiring support include tomatoes, pole beans, cucumbers, climbing peas, small melons, and winter squash.

Single stakes can be used to tie up tomatoes or for pole beans to vine around. Heavy-duty cages made from concrete reinforcing wire or livestock panels provide more stable options for large vining tomato varieties. A-frame trellises look beautiful in raised and in-ground beds and are perfect for pole beans, climbing peas, and cucumbers. Arch trellises, the sweethearts of vertical gardening, support cucumbers, small melons, climbing peas, winter squash, and pole beans.

Livestock panel is a versatile option. Using only T-posts to keep it upright, it offers enough structure for most vining plants. Trimmed with bolt cutters, it can be made into wire cages for tomato plants. Another popular option is to bend it into an arch trellis, anchored with T-posts or secured between two raised beds.

But for those with simpler tastes, two sticks or poles placed in the ground or near your containers with twine woven between them is a perfect pea, bean, or cucumber support structure.

Bamboo works well for just about any vertical gardening project. A fun option for kids is to take pieces of bamboo and arrange them into a tepee shape. Grow pole beans around each pole and let the children play inside the "tepee."

When choosing your vertical support, consider the sprawling or vining nature of the plant. Beans prefer vertical "poles" and will grow up them on their own. Peas and cucumbers enjoy horizontal support for their tendrils to latch on to. Winter squash and cucumbers need a bit of "training," so as they grow, you may need to weave the growing stem around the nearest support. Tomatoes must be tied up or propped up, otherwise they will grow along the ground. Knowing these growth habits will help you choose the best option for incorporating vertical gardening into your plan.

How to Build a Raised Bed Garden

You can find a myriad of options and plans for building a raised bed, but I'll share the most basic plan.

Preparing Your Site

The most important part of preparing your site is making sure it is level. Measure out the bed size and check its slope with a leveling tool. If there is any slope to the ground, you may need to scrape one side until the land is level on all sides.

If your ground contains pernicious weeds or grass, lay down an organic barrier, such as cardboard, to smother them. An alternative is to simply scrape the top layer of vegetation and turn it over; it will compost into the soil over time. If you think you may have rodents such as voles or moles, you will need a permanent barrier (hardware cloth, for example) because organic barriers will eventually break down into the soil.

Materials and Tools Needed

If you're willing to pay for convenience, purchasing raised bed kits is an option. But to save money and go the DIY route, you'll need these tools to construct a standard 4-by-8-foot, 10-inch-high raised bed:

- 3 (2-by-10-inch-by-8-foot) pieces of lumber (or 2 by 8 inches or 2 by 12 inches, depending on how tall you want your beds)
- Measuring tape
- Pencil
- Carpenter's square
- Circular saw or handsaw
- Drill or impact driver
- 12 (2½-inch) deck screws
- Roll of ¼-inch hardware cloth (optional)
- Staple gun (optional)
- Level

The most durable and budget-friendly wood is pressure-treated pine, widely available at home supply stores. However, there is a lack of research showing whether chemicals used in the treatment process leach into the soil and at what levels (if any) those chemicals are taken up by plants. You can check with your local home center or lumberyard to find out what rot-resistant natural wood options are available.

Building Your Raised Bed

Once you gather the materials, set aside a few hours to build your raised bed. Though it can be built by one person, an extra set of hands is always useful.

1. Take one 8-foot board and mark it with the pencil 4 feet from the end. Use a carpenter's square to draw a vertical line across the board.

2. Cut the board at the vertical line with a saw.

3. Lay out the four pieces of board in the shape of a rectangle: the two 8-foot sections parallel to each other and the two 4-foot sections parallel to each other.

4. Situate one 8-foot board perpendicular to one 4-foot board, where their ends meet flush. Position the other corners of the raised bed the same way.

5. Using the drill, pre-drill the holes. Then, screw each of the four corners together where the boards meet, using three deck screws per corner.

6. If you're using hardware cloth to cover the bottom of the bed (this prevents ground-dwelling rodents from getting to your plants from underneath), spread the cloth over the bed, stapling it in place. If it doesn't cover the entire bed and you have to use two strips, make sure you have a 6-inch overlap between strips.

7. Carry the bed to its site and position it. Set the level on each of the four sides, ensuring the bed is level in all directions. If the bed isn't level, use a shovel to scrape down higher areas of dirt until the bed is level.

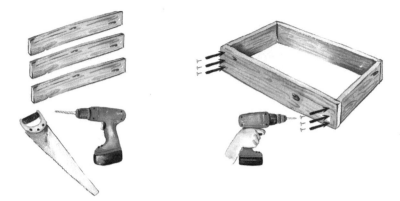

These plans can be modified for differing dimensions, but you should never exceed 4 feet in width. You want to be able to reach into the middle of the bed. If your bed will be next to a fence or other area, make it no wider than 3 feet. The length of the bed is up to you.

Many people prefer taller raised beds. For a bed taller than 12 inches, you will need more than one board for each side. In this case, each corner will need to be anchored by a 4-by-4-inch post, with each side board screwed into the post instead of into the perpendicular side board.

Filling and Sectioning Your Raised Bed

For a raised bed, you want a slightly "heavier" medium (soil mixture) than for a container garden. A higher proportion of topsoil and compost adds moisture retention and nutrients. We will explore raised bed soil mixes later in this chapter.

As you begin planting your vegetables (see chapter 4), think about the orientation of your raised bed, especially in regard to larger and taller plants.

Plants that grow vertically or taller than others should be planted on the north, east, or northeast part of your raised bed. Lower-growing plants should go on the south, west, or southwest side. This way, tall crops, such as tomatoes or pole beans, do not shade shorter crops, such as peppers or sweet potatoes, from the much-needed southwesterly sun exposure. The exception is if you plan to grow cool-weather crops, such as greens, further into the summer. These crops benefit from afternoon shade and may grow longer before bolting if provided with shade. (For gardeners in the southern hemisphere, these cardinal directions will be opposite.)

How to Cover Your Garden

Most gardens will benefit from some type of covering to protect them from the elements during at least part of the year.

Floating row covers help gardeners begin their growing season earlier and extend it later. Air- and water-permeable covers made from lightweight polyester fabric protect crops from frost, allowing a few extra weeks of growing time on the bookends of the season. For in-ground gardens and raised beds, you can make arches with PVC pipe and lay the cover on top for a dome effect. Attach the cover to the PVC with clamps to ensure it doesn't blow off. For small plantings or for those in containers, placing upside-down plastic pots or cups on top of vulnerable plants works well. (Place a rock on top of the pot or cup to prevent it from blowing away.)

In some areas, wind damage is a major concern. Siting your garden on the south or southwest side of a structure or natural brush offers some protection. Well-anchored floating row covers can also protect lower-growing or young crops from wind.

Many gardeners find their biggest challenge isn't the cold or wind, but heat. Particularly in the southern United States, the recommended full-sun location might translate to stressed plants when temperatures rise to almost 100°F. In this case, afternoon shade can help sun-loving crops such as tomatoes and peppers. If you grow in containers, move them to a shady location in the heat of the day. If you grow in raised beds or an in-ground garden, use shade cloths in place of floating row covers (floating row covers trap heat; shade cloths allow air circulation).

For other conditions necessitating extra protection, always consider your plants' particular needs when deciding how to best cover your garden.

How to Make Your Own Soil Mix

The biggest advantage to growing in containers or raised beds is that you can control the soil medium.

The soil for both types of gardens contains many of the same ingredients, with slight variations. Therefore, my soil mix recipes vary. With containers, drainage is critical, because soggy soil will cause rot and plant death, which is why you should never put garden soil in containers. Raised beds, on the other hand, benefit from the moisture-holding capacity of garden soil.

Many online soil mix recipes contain a diverse range of ingredients, and although diversity is good, it's more important at this stage for soil making to be practical, inexpensive, and doable.

Here is a list of common soil components, available in most garden centers or online:

- **Coconut coir:** an alternative to peat moss serving the same function but with a neutral pH
- **Compost:** final product of decayed living matter that adds fertility; can be purchased or homemade
- **Peat moss:** organic material derived from peat bogs that holds moisture and nutrients and contributes to the structure and tilth of soil, but has a low pH
- **Perlite:** volcanic glass expanded through heat that adds aeration
- **Vermiculite:** a combination of heat-expanded minerals that adds aeration while increasing water retention

Container Soil Mix

3 parts peat moss or coconut coir

3 parts finished compost

2 parts perlite

1 part vermiculite

This forms the base. I recommend adding up to 1 part worm castings or up to ¼ part slow-release organic fertilizer. If you use peat moss, add 1 ounce of dolomitic lime for every 1 gallon of peat (do not do this if planting potatoes).

Raised Bed Soil Mix

1 part topsoil (bagged or native)

1 part finished compost (homemade, bulk compost, or OMRI-certified bagged)

1 part other organic materials

For the 1 part other organic materials, I've had success using peat moss, vermiculite, composted chicken manure, and worm castings. Other options include greensand, biochar, coconut coir (in place of peat moss), and perlite.

As you can see, you have some flexibility. The key is to include materials that offer both water retention and drainage, as well as rich organic material. If all this overwhelms you, however, go for bagged mixes, though I recommend choosing organic blends for the long-term health of your garden.

Compost and Mulch

To keep your garden thriving year after year, you will want to invest in compost and mulch.

You can make your own compost from kitchen vegetable scraps, shredded paper, grass clippings, fallen leaves, eggshells, weeds, and other organic materials.

Building your own compost pile can be as simple or as complex as you want. Some people pile the composting materials in their yard and turn over the pile every week or so. Others purchase or make their own composting bin setup. But unless you make a lot of compost or you grow a tiny garden, you might find you can't produce as much as you need. In that case, you can purchase bagged compost or buy it in bulk from local landscaping companies. Some local municipalities also offer free compost if you can load and transport it yourself. Whatever you choose, compost contributes to the short- and long-term health and vitality of your garden.

Mulch is another important material no garden should be without. A layer of mulch on your raised bed, containers, or in-ground garden serves multiple purposes. First, a 2-inch layer of mulch prevents most weed seeds from sprouting. This means less weeding for you and less competition for nutrients and water for your plants. Second, mulch regulates moisture. In times of too much rain, mulch works like a sponge and absorbs excess water, releasing it as the area surrounding it dries out. In times of drought, mulch prevents evaporation and retains moisture in the soil for longer. Organic mulch, such as shredded fallen leaves, wood chips, and straw, breaks down into the soil, enriching it.

The best way to obtain mulch is to harvest it from your own yard. If you have deciduous trees, collect their leaves in the fall, store them in bags, shred them using a lawn mower or leaf shredder, and put them on top of your soil in the spring. In the absence of enough fallen leaves, wood chips are another great source. Many tree services will deliver freshly ground wood chips to your door if they're in the area; you just have to call and ask. You can also buy bagged mulch at the garden center. Avoid colored mulch for your vegetable garden, though, because some of the cheaper options contain dyes that could be harmful for your plants. Another option is straw, which you can usually get from a garden center or farmers' co-op. Whichever option you choose, keep the mulch at the surface; don't till or incorporate mulch into the soil.

FAQ: Building a Garden

Can I use wood from an old fence or deck to build my raised bed?
Pressure-treated wood manufactured prior to 2003 contains chromated copper arsenate (CCA), which isn't considered safe for vegetable gardens. In 2003, the pressure-treating process changed to alkaline copper quaternary (ACQ), which the Environmental Protection Agency considers a safe alternative. It's a personal decision, whether to use pressure-treated wood, but if you do, I recommend staying away from any manufactured prior to 2003.

What containers are best for vegetables? Terra-cotta clay pots may seem like an ideal choice, but they actually dry out faster because of their porous surface. Plastic pots and buckets retain moisture better and weigh less. With proper drainage, these can be excellent choices. Wood and metal containers are also options. Metal will last longer, but it will heat up. This can be good for heat-loving plants but detrimental to plants needing cooler soil conditions. And although wood may seem cumbersome because of its weight, it allows breathability and will last for years. Grow bags are portable, storable, and affordable. They allow drainage and air exchange critical to the health of plant roots, while retaining moisture like plastic pots do.

Can I use hay as mulch? Organic hay is an excellent mulch; it covers well and adds nutritious organic matter to soil as it breaks down. However, it can be hard to find. The more commonly found hay usually contains the broadleaf weed killer aminopyralid, which, if applied to your garden, can make your plants abnormally curled and stunted. Worse, the chemicals persist in the soil for years.

Will adding gravel to the bottom of my containers increase drainage?
Contrary to popular belief, placing gravel or rocks in the bottom of a pot does not improve drainage. Instead, having less soil in the pot (because of the addition of gravel) causes the soil to get even more waterlogged. In order to maintain a healthy level of drainage, ensure the pots have drainage holes at the bottom and include drainage-increasing amendments, such as perlite, in the potting soil.

How often should I refresh my raised bed soil? Each year, preferably twice—once in the spring and once in the fall—you should plan to add 1 to 2 inches of compost to the top of your raised beds. Existing soil life will begin breaking down the compost, enriching the soil from the top down into the root zone.

Can I reuse potting soil year after year? As long as your plants didn't suffer from disease the previous season, you can reuse some of the soil. Plan to amend roughly half the container's volume with new potting mix each time you plant a new planting. Dump the soil from your containers into a wheelbarrow and add amendments, such as worm castings, compost, perlite, and slow-release fertilizer, for nutrition and drainage. Moisten the mix, stir it well, and return it to the containers.

CHAPTER FOUR

Planting Your Vegetable Garden

It's important to know the basics of planting so you can get your baby plants off to their best start. In this chapter we cover general principles for starting seeds indoors, transplanting into the garden, and direct sowing seeds. Some plants thrive when planted one way or another, and those nuances will be covered in the profiles in part 2.

Starting Seeds Indoors

Although many first-time gardeners choose to purchase transplants and direct sow seeds, some want to start seeds indoors. With an understanding of the basics and following the outlined steps, you can give your plants a healthy start.

Most seeds are started indoors 4 to 6 weeks prior to the transplanting date; however, some seeds require more time (e.g., peppers) and some less (e.g., squash and other cucurbits). See part 2 for the specific dates for starting different plants.

Plant two seeds per cell. If both germinate, snip the weaker seedling at soil level after the second set of leaves appears. (The first leaves to appear are cotyledons, not actual leaves. They will eventually die off after several sets of "true" leaves form.)

A healthy seedling will be compact and stocky. If you notice a seedling growing tall and turning toward the light, the light levels aren't sufficient. If you're using a grow light, bring the seedlings closer to the light. If the seedling suddenly wilts and dies, it likely had a condition called "damping off," which is a fungal disease present in the soil. Start seeds with a bagged seed-starting mix, using new or sterile containers, to avoid this problem.

When the seedlings grow more than twice the height of the container, prepare to either transfer the plant to a larger container or plant it in the garden if possible. Plants will suffer if they remain for too long in a container that is too small, and if they survive until transplanting, they'll have a harder time adjusting.

To start growing seeds:

1. Gather seed packets, seed-starting supplies (see page 12), large bowl, serving spoon, watering can or large cup, spray bottle, and plastic wrap.

2. Pour your seed-starting mix into the large bowl, leaving about 1 cup of mix in the bag. Add enough water to the bowl to moisten the seed-starting mixture. Mix well.

3. Scoop moistened seed-starting mix into a seed-starting tray or container. Fill to within ¼ inch of the top. Place the tray or container inside a second tray (seed-starting kits come with this; otherwise, use a rimmed baking sheet).

4. Place two seeds per cell on top of the mix. Tamp down slightly, and except for the largest seeds (e.g., peas or squash), do not bury the seed.

5. Label the cells or groups of cells with the type and variety of seed.

6. Sprinkle the reserved 1 cup of seed-starting mix on top of the seed to barely cover it.

7. Using a spray bottle, mist the new seed-starting mix until thoroughly moistened.

8. If your seed-starting tray has a dome, cover the tray with it. If there is no dome, spread a layer of plastic wrap on top of the containers. Poke a few holes in the top with a toothpick.

9. Check on your seeds every couple of days, misting again if the top of the soil begins to dry out. With a dome or plastic wrap in place, this may not be necessary for several days, if at all.

10. When the first seedlings appear, remove the dome or plastic wrap and immediately place the tray just a few inches under a grow light. Keep the grow light on for 16 hours per day. Mist your seedlings daily.

11. When the second set of leaves appears (the first "true" leaves), begin watering the trays from the bottom, filling the tray with ¼ inch of water. (Watering young seedlings from the top can damage their stems.)

12. As the seedlings grow, move the grow light up, keeping the tops of the plants 4 to 6 inches from the light. Keep the soil moist but not water-logged. If you water from the bottom and the soil hasn't taken up all the water within an hour, remove excess water with a turkey baster, or pour it off carefully.

Using Recycled Materials to Start Seeds

Although you can purchase seed-starting trays and seed-starting kits, you can also repurpose existing materials. Here are some great options.

Plant pots. If you planted flowers or vegetables last year and kept the containers, use them. Just be sure to sterilize them with a 10 percent bleach mixture.

Newspaper pots. Wrap newspaper strips around soup cans and tape the strips together to secure them. Then, remove the can and you have a seed-starting pot that you can transplant directly into the ground when ready.

Plastic cups or yogurt containers. With holes poked in the bottom, plastic cups are an excellent option.

Toilet paper rolls. Cut the cardboard rolls in half and fold the bottom under to create a stable base. Toilet paper rolls can transplant directly into the garden, but because they don't break down into the soil quickly, you should unfold the bottom before transplanting them.

Although cute, eggshells or egg cartons are not good options because the root systems of most plants require more space than eggshells or cartons allow.

Transplanting Seedlings

Purchased transplants or baby plants grown from seed indoors need special care when being transplanted.

The first critical step is to ensure the seedlings are ready for the outdoors, or "hardened off." Most transplants you purchase have lived outside under sunlight and are ready to go into the garden, but seedlings you grew from seed require an extra step.

Just as a mother introduces her baby to solid foods little by little, you want to introduce your seedlings to the outdoors gradually. For 1 to 2 weeks prior to transplanting, take the seedlings outside for increasing amounts of time per day, starting with one hour and working up to a full day and night. At first, place them somewhere shady and protected from wind. Gradually work up to full sun (start with morning sun, then afternoon sun) and more of a breeze. *This step is extremely important.* Just a few extra hours of afternoon sunlight or one windy day can stunt or kill your seedlings.

When the seedlings are ready to be transplanted, gather your supplies: full watering can, trowel, stool or kneeling pad, gloves, and seedlings.

1. Set the transplants in your garden area or container, on top of the soil, to get a visual idea of the spacing. Measure if necessary.

2. Using a trowel, dig a hole the depth of the planting container. (For tomatoes, dig a deeper hole; see the tomato profile on page 126 for more information.)

3. Fill the hole halfway with water. If it drains quickly, fill it again.

4. Place the transplant in the planting hole, backfilling with the soil you removed from the hole. Tamp down the soil around the plant gently but firmly, taking care not to damage the stem or compress the soil.

5. Water again from the top until the soil around the transplant is saturated.

When is the proper time to transplant? First, your seedlings must be ready. Ideally, there should be at least three sets of true leaves. Second, check your average last-frost date and make sure you're planting a particular plant at the correct time relative to that date. Third, even if the calendar says it's time to plant, observe your local weather conditions and check your long-range forecast. If in doubt, wait.

How to Read a Seed Packet

Whether you start seeds indoors or direct sow, get familiar with the details on seed packets. Although each seed supplier prints slight variations, most packets include the following information:

Kind/variety: what vegetable or herb it is, along with the particular variety.

Description: how the plant grows or what kind of harvest it produces.

Days to maturity: the average number of days the plant needs to grow from the time it is planted in the garden to full maturity. This can vary based on local conditions. Knowing this date helps with succession planting and when you need a plant to harvest before the first fall frost.

Quantity: how many seeds or weight of seeds in ounces or grams per seed pack. This helps you know how many seed packets to purchase.

Planting instructions: directions on proper sowing depth and spacing, as well as optimum planting time relative to frost or soil temperature. Some will include trellis requirements if applicable and harvest instructions.

Date: when the seeds were packaged. Most seeds will last for a few years or longer under the right conditions, but the newer the seeds, the better the germination rate will be.

Description

Spinach does well with cool weather, short days, high soil fertility, ample moisture, and neutral pH (6.5–7.5).

Date

Kind/Variety

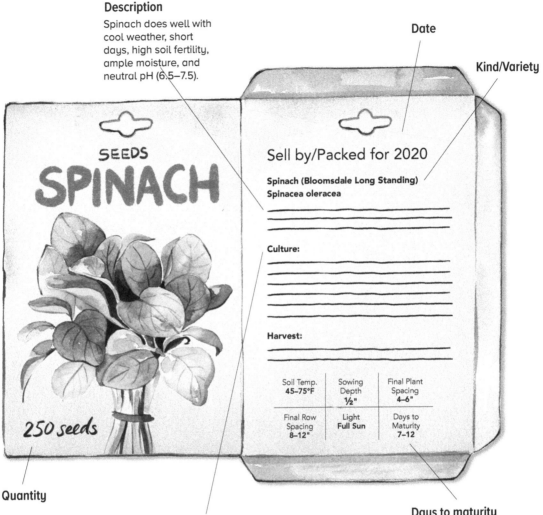

Sell by/Packed for 2020

Spinach (Bloomsdale Long Standing)
Spinacea oleracea

_____
_____

Culture:
_____
_____
_____
_____

Harvest:
_____

Soil Temp. 45–75°F	Sowing Depth ½"	Final Plant Spacing 4–6"
Final Row Spacing 8–12"	Light **Full Sun**	Days to Maturity 7–12

Quantity

250 seeds

Days to maturity

Planting instructions

Culture: Direct sow in spring as soon as the ground can be worked. Thin at 3–4 true leaves. Plant successions every 2 weeks. Mulch. For fall and winter greens, direct sow 1 month before first frost (sow thickly if grasshoppers are a problem). Heat can kill the seedings, so wait for cool weather. Frosts sweeten the flavor. May tolerate temperatures as low as 0°F. Protect with row cover and mulch as necessary. Overwintered spinach will resume growth in the spring.

Harvest: Snip off leaves near the base or harvest whole plants when hot weather threatens.

Direct Sowing

Many vegetables grow best when their seeds are planted directly in the garden or container. Beans, peas, cucumbers, squash, okra, corn, and melons germinate rapidly in warm soil and thrive when their roots are never disrupted by transplanting. Other crops, such as lettuce and greens, can be transplanted, but it's just as easy to direct sow. Still others, such as carrots and beets, prefer staying in one spot where their roots can sink in quickly and deeply.

Most direct sow seeds are planted in rows. Here's how to do it in your garden or container:

1. Prior to planting, loosen the top few inches of soil with a rake (for garden beds) or three-pronged fork (for containers) and work in organic matter such as compost, if you haven't already.

2. Using the corner of a hoe (for larger seeds), the prongs of a rake (for smaller seeds), or your fingers (for containers), prepare an indented row twice the depth of the seed.

3. Drop seeds into the row at the recommended spacing.

4. Gently backfill the row with soil to cover the seeds completely, tamping the soil down gently.

5. Irrigate with a fine mist of water until the soil is saturated.

Some seeds are fine when planted with less precision. Scatter tiny seeds such as carrots and lettuce on top of the soil and run your fingers or rake across the soil to let the seeds settle in without getting buried too deeply. They can—and often prefer to—germinate with access to sunlight. Just keep the planting area moist until germination.

Other seeds benefit from a bit of coaxing to help them germinate faster. Soak hard-coated seeds such as beans and okra in water for several hours to soften the seed coat. Although this step is not necessary, it can hasten germination.

Seeds will germinate at the highest rate when they're planted at the ideal time. The soil temperature is the biggest indicator of the ideal planting time. Many seed packets include the ideal soil temperature, but you can find this information in part 2 or online. Planting into soggy soil will cause many seeds of summer crops to rot. Assuming the soil temperature is ideal, wait until the soil is fairly moist and time your planting before a rain.

FAQ: Seed Starting and Planting

How do I know when to start seeds indoors? In part 2 you will find seed-sowing recommendations relative to your average last frost. Some plants germinate and grow faster than others, and the best time to transplant them outside also varies. For example, tomato seeds are usually planted indoors 6 to 8 weeks before the average last frost. Pepper seeds typically need 10 to 12 weeks of indoor growing time, but because they thrive when transplanted 2 to 4 weeks later than tomatoes, tomato and pepper seeds can be sown at the same time. It may seem complicated, but with a little experience it will become easy.

How long does it take for seeds to germinate? Germination rate varies by plant and with climatic conditions. Most seeds planted in a controlled indoor environment will germinate within 7 to 10 days. Pepper seeds can take longer; placing these in a warm area (on top of a dryer, refrigerator, or seedling heat mat) will speed up the process. Outside, soil temperature is the biggest predictor of germination time. The same bean or squash seed planted in spring soil that is 70° may take a week to germinate, whereas a succession planting in summer soil that is 85° could germinate in 2 to 3 days.

What should I do to keep my indoor seedlings healthy? Do not overwater; roots need oxygen, too. Turn on a gentle fan to help strengthen seedling stems. Above all, keep plants within a few inches of a grow light. If you find your seedlings growing tall and thin (known as "leggy") and stretching toward a light source, your plant is stressed for light. This is the most common seed-starting mistake I see, and sadly, once a plant is stressed this way, it's hard for it to rebound. Prevent this by ensuring your seedlings get plenty of light.

Will my seedlings stay in the original containers until I plant them outside? As a general rule, if the height of the plant doubles the height of the container, the plant needs more room. If this happens and it's not yet time to transplant, you can "pot up" the plant, which means transplanting it into a larger container. If you used shallow seed-starting trays, you can pot up to a plastic cup with drainage holes. When potting up, it's good to use a potting mix instead of a seed-starting mix because plants at this stage can use the extra fertilization a potting mix provides.

If I'm planting in containers, can I start seeds indoors in those containers and later move them outside? In theory, yes, though the size and weight of most containers (and the limitations of indoor grow light space) might make this impractical. Small pots of herbs or lettuce are good options if you want to skip transplanting.

Should I add anything to the planting hole when transplanting? A common recommendation for years was to add extra fertilizer and compost to the planting hole. A better plan is to ensure the entire planting medium is full of organic matter. This encourages roots to grow deeper and wider, which results in stronger, more resilient plants.

All my seeds germinated! I planted more than I needed; now what do I do? You need to cull extra seedlings. We all hate to do it, but if you skip this step, seedlings will compete for water and nutrients and none will thrive. Take scissors and snip the weaker plant at soil level so you don't disturb the delicate root system of the remaining seedling. This is necessary for both indoor and outdoor sowings.

CHAPTER FIVE

Maintaining and Harvesting Your Vegetable Garden

For a beginning gardener, planning and planting the garden requires much thought and attention. After clearing those hurdles, it's not uncommon to look at the garden and think, "Now what?" In this chapter, we discuss the important tasks you need to do throughout the season to maintain your garden, from how to water to harvesting your vegetables.

Watering Your Garden

Whether you live in a drought-prone area or a climate that receives above-average rainfall, you'll need to provide supplemental irrigation for your garden. It's best to plan your irrigation method at planting time or soon after.

In a small raised bed garden or a container garden, hand-watering with watering cans or a hose may be enough. However, this requires hands-on attentiveness and labor that you may not want to commit to throughout the gardening season. Also, overhead watering compounds fungal diseases that thrive in wet and humid conditions.

Many gardeners opt for irrigation systems such as soaker hoses or drip emitters. With these methods, water goes directly into the soil, so less water is lost to evaporation.

Soaker hoses work great in raised beds because they leach water throughout the length of the hose, saturating the raised bed evenly. They are especially good in beds with closely spaced plants such as carrots, beets, lettuce, greens, and onions.

Drip emitter systems work well in all types of gardens. The drip lines leach water about every 18 inches. They are easy to install, and you can configure and add to your drip system as your garden expands. For containers, lines fitted with isolated "spot" emitters provide one source of water per container.

For either soaker hoses or drip systems, I recommend investing in an inexpensive timer fitted to your water spigot so you can set when and for how long your garden receives water. Because each system leaches water slowly, it's best to leave it on for a couple of hours per watering. My garden is on a timer to receive water from 5:00 a.m. to 7:00 a.m. every 3 to 4 days during peak season. My timer has a "rain delay" function that allows me to postpone the scheduled watering if we receive rainfall.

Generally speaking, most vegetables and herbs in an in-ground or raised bed garden thrive with an average of 1 inch of water per week. Investing in a rain gauge will help you track when supplemental irrigation is necessary.

Container plants require more water because of the well-draining requirements of container soil. Because plants show the same symptoms of droopy, wilting leaves both when overwatered and underwatered, a rain gauge and a moisture meter will help you assess water-related issues during the growing season.

How to Check Your Soil Quality

For in-ground gardens and raised beds where you're adding compost or top-soil, I recommend testing your soil once per year. If you fill your raised beds or containers with a commercial soil mix (or the soil mix on page 45), you may still want to check your soil quality from time to time, especially if your plants don't perform as expected.

A soil test reveals the composition of your soil (sand, silt, clay, or loam), the pH level, and the levels of important nutrients. You can purchase soil-testing kits at your local garden center, or you can send a soil sample to an independent laboratory or to a lab through your local cooperative extension service.

To get an accurately representative soil sample, dig six small holes in your garden area in a zigzag pattern, removing any grass or weeds on top. Take a vertical section from each hole the length of the trowel and place it in a clean plastic bucket. Mix the soil from all six spots and scoop out the amount required for a soil test, usually around 2 cups. For a professional soil test, follow the laboratory's instructions on bagging and shipping (if necessary).

I've found the home soil-testing kits perform decently at providing a general idea of the pH and nutrient levels, but a professional soil test offers more detailed insight. A professional test report also provides recommendations for amending the soil, should it be nutrient deficient or out of pH balance. Beware, though: Some of these recommendations are not organic, so do your research for organic options or specifically request organic options from the lab.

Moisture meters sometimes come with a built-in pH meter. In my experience, these are helpful for giving you a range only, such as if your soil is highly acidic or alkaline. For more specific pH testing, opt for a professional soil test.

Maintaining Your Garden

Although no garden will live up to a wide-eyed new gardener's expectations (no matter what you do, you will battle weeds and pests), these tips will help keep your garden as healthy as possible.

Walk your garden daily. Checking your garden daily, even without working in it, lets you keep an eye on growth and potential issues. Diseases and pests can rapidly overtake untended gardens, but with early intervention, you can limit the damage.

Handpick pests. Get to know the most common pests—aphids, squash bugs, hornworms, bean beetles, cucumber beetles, cabbage worms, etc.—and handpick any you see. Before resorting to spray (organic or not), try to manually remove them. Grab garden gloves and a bucket of water (with a drop of dish soap to cut the surface tension of the water), and drop the pests into the bucket.

Don't kill a bug you can't identify. Most insects in your garden are beneficial or harmless. If in doubt, leave it alone; many beneficial insects prey on bad ones. An Internet search will come in handy, as will Facebook gardening groups, where experienced gardeners can help you identify an insect. Good bugs include ladybugs, lacewings, syrphid flies or hoverflies, ground beetles, assassin bugs, and spiders.

Add flowers. To attract beneficial insects, add flowers and allow bolted plants to flower. Great flowers to add include cosmos, calendula, nasturtium, sunflowers, yarrow, zinnia, and alyssum. Bolted lettuce, arugula, carrots, and onions develop flowers that attract beneficial insects in droves, as do herbs such as oregano, parsley, cilantro, and thyme. With a suitable habitat, these beneficial insects will keep many pest insects in check. For example, I rarely have to spray for aphids because the ladybugs, lacewings, and syrphid flies take care of them for me.

Mulch. Don't delay mulching. As soon as plants reach about 6 inches high, add a 2-inch layer of mulch for weed control and moisture conservation.

Weed regularly. Even with mulch, some weed sprouts break through. Set it on your calendar to weed at least weekly. Once weeds get out of hand, it's much more difficult to catch up.

Water in the morning. Whether you hand-water or use a drip irrigation system, water in the morning hours. This gives the plants the moisture they need at the ideal time, plus it limits evaporation and cuts down on fungal diseases that commonly spread with evening watering.

Fertilize, if necessary. Many new gardens do not require supplemental fertilization at first, but as plants take up nutrients in the soil, additional fertilizer can help. Fish emulsion is an effective organic and low-dose source of nitrogen. This helps plants in their early developmental stages develop the leaves needed for photosynthesis. Too much nitrogen can cause fruiting plants to produce lots of foliage and little fruit. If your plants are growing rapidly, skip the nitrogen fertilizer. But if they appear stunted, this low-dose form of nitrogen can help. In my raised bed gardens, I add fish emulsion every 2 weeks to my fruiting plants until they start developing flowers.

Prune diseased foliage. The most common plant diseases are fungal diseases. These don't kill the plant right away, but they can if left unchecked. Yellow leaves at the bottom of tomato plants usually signal early blight, and a white powder on squash and cucumber leaves indicates powdery mildew. Prune affected leaves and stems immediately and dispose of them in the trash (not compost). You can remove up to 25 percent of a plant's leaves. When you catch disease early, you can lessen its spread.

Train vertical plants to their trellises. Plants such as beans and peas usually train themselves, but others, such as cucumbers and vining tomatoes, need some help. Every few days, gently wrap cucumber vines around the trellis in a zigzag pattern. Lift tomato vines and situate them on the correct rung of a tomato cage or tie them to whatever trellis you use. It's important to keep all vines spaced out for proper airflow as you train them.

These small maintenance steps will keep your garden as healthy as possible. But bear in mind, when using organic practices, it takes time for healthy insect populations and healthy soil to build up. Don't expect perfection in the first season, but instead look for progress.

Common Problems and Pests and What to Do about Them

Each organic garden will experience different problems and pests throughout the growing season, and until you start gardening, you won't know which ones you'll encounter. These are some of the most common issues.

Early blight or Septoria leaf spot on tomatoes. These fungal diseases cause yellowing leaves starting at the bottom of a tomato plant. Early blight may look like a target, with outer circles of yellow darkening to brown in the center. Septoria leaf spot appears as many brown dots on leaves and often shows up later in the season. Cut off and dispose of all affected stems when the leaves aren't wet. During rainy periods, you may have to do this daily to get it under control.

Powdery mildew. Most common on squash, zucchini, and cucumbers, powdery mildew is a fungal disease that looks like white powder on the tops of leaves. Left unchecked, it will spread up the plant and inhibit photosynthesis and subsequent fruit production. If you catch it early, clip off affected leaves, up to 25 percent of the plant. If that doesn't work, mix 1 teaspoon of baking soda with 1 quart of water and spray on affected and unaffected leaves once a week.

Blossom-end rot. Most common on tomatoes, this black rotted spot appears where the blossom drops off the fruit. It can also affect squash, melons, and peppers. Although this condition is caused by a plant's inability to take up calcium from the soil, simply adding calcium is usually not the best remedy. Most soils have enough calcium present (a soil test will confirm this); the problem typically lies in uneven watering or out-of-balance pH. Keep plants watered regularly, especially during the blossoming and fruiting stages. If this doesn't help, get a soil test to determine if a lack of calcium or pH issue is to blame.

Lack of pollination. When a fruit stops growing and begins to rot, usually a lack of pollination is the cause. Squash, zucchini, cucumbers, and melons are most susceptible to this condition. Without the presence of pollinators such as bees, cross-pollinating plants can't develop fruit. You may need to hand-pollinate. Find the male flower (the one without a fruit developing at the base) and with a cotton swab transfer the pollen from its stamen onto the flower of the female (the one with a fruit at the base). These flowers only open once per day, usually in the morning, so you'll need to go out early, and daily.

Aphids. Tiny, pear-shaped insects in various colors, aphids congregate on new growth of many plants such as tomatoes and peppers, especially early in the season. Avoid spraying, because most insecticidal soaps also kill ladybug, lacewing, and syrphid fly larvae, which prey upon aphids. Instead, apply worm castings to the base of the plants and water well. Worm castings contain chitinase, an enzyme that aphids cannot digest. When the aphids suck the plant juices containing chitinase, they die.

Worms. Cabbage worms, tomato hornworms, armyworms, and other worms can defoliate your vegetable plants almost overnight. If handpicking doesn't keep them under control, coat affected crops with the organic pesticide *Bacillus thuringiensis*, being careful to avoid any flowers. You might also consider a floating row cover to protect vulnerable crops (broccoli, cabbage, kale, and lettuce) against the moths that lay the eggs that hatch into these worms.

Beetles. Beetles such as squash bugs, stinkbugs, Japanese bean beetles, Mexican bean beetles, cucumber beetles, and others are some of the most difficult pests to control. Organic options are limited, because deterrents that might affect these beetles will also kill beneficial beetles such as ground beetles and ladybugs. The best way to control these pests is to handpick adults and remove egg clusters. Removing infested plants and practicing crop rotation also help for future seasons.

Less is more when it comes to issues in an organic garden. Early manual removal of diseased plants and pests offers the best protection. Be willing to accept some damage, and know that the healthier the soil is, the healthier the plants will be, which enables them to withstand more pest and disease damage over the course of the season.

Harvesting and Storing Your Produce

You've worked hard on planning, planting, and maintaining your garden, and now harvest time is approaching. What to do?

First, you need to know when a vegetable or herb is ready to harvest. Some crops have a short window for optimum harvest—sometimes only one day! Corn, okra, and squash fall into this category. Specifics are listed in the plant profiles in part 2. The time of day to harvest is also worth considering. Herbs are usually best harvested in the morning after the dew dries off. Vegetables can be harvested any time of day, though I recommend not harvesting when foliage is wet, simply so you can avoid spreading disease via drops of water.

Some crops are easily picked by hand, such as peas, green beans, cantaloupe, some tomatoes, and leafy greens. Grasp the stem with one hand and the vegetable or fruit with the other and snap it off. Others, such as peppers, cucumbers, watermelon, yellow squash, and okra, require cutting the stem just above the fruit with pruning shears or micro-tip pruners. By doing this you'll avoid damaging the plant. Larger-stemmed vegetables such as zucchini, broccoli, and cabbage are best cut with a knife. Use a trowel to harvest root crops such as carrots, beets, garlic, potatoes, sweet potatoes, and onions. Dig straight down a few inches away from the plant and loosen the soil, being careful not to nick the vegetable underground (if you do, eat it within a few days).

And if you harvest more than you can eat? Most popular preserving options include canning, freezing, and dehydrating. Though these methods of preservation each have a slight learning curve, they are easily grasped.

What to Do at the End of the Growing Season

Toward the end of your growing season, your garden may look worn out. You might be feeling the same! But before you and your garden take a well-deserved winter break, set your garden up for success next season.

Remove all diseased and pest-infested plants. Removing them from the garden reduces the chance of compounding infestation next season.

Feel free to leave nondiseased plants in raised beds or in-ground gardens. Though you might not prefer the aesthetics, leaving some plants can boost productivity next season. Root networks decompose naturally, feeding soil life. Beneficial insects can overwinter in plant debris. Large plants with deep taproots, such as okra, do not budge easily in the fall but will come out with a one-handed tug in the spring.

Cover the soil on raised beds and in-ground gardens. Do not leave your soil bare over the winter. The most nutritious layer of the soil is found in the top few inches, and uncovered soil erodes in heavy winter rains and snow. Add a layer of compost on top to replenish nutrients, or at the very least leave the mulch on top to protect the soil and break down over the winter.

Empty containers, sterilize them, and put them away. Containers left out in the elements over the winter may crack and degrade. Place soil from nondiseased plants in a large bin with a lid. You can reuse this soil next season combined with some fresh soil mixture. Clean the empty containers with a 10 percent bleach mixture to kill any remaining pathogens. Store the containers in a sheltered location.

FAQ: Garden Maintenance and Harvest

When irrigating, how do I know how much water my garden receives? Whereas many gardeners just eye their plants to make sure the water provided meets their needs, others want to measure it. The easiest way to do this is to place a 1-inch-deep container (e.g., a tuna can) below a drip emitter or under a soaker hose. When the container fills, your garden has received 1 inch of water.

Do I place soaker hoses or drip lines above or below the mulch? Either. When placed below the mulch, water will go directly to the plants, but you also risk inadvertently slicing into the lines when working the soil with a hoe. Lines placed on top of the mulch can be easily moved if you see certain plants in need of more or less water.

What are my options for organic soil amendments? If your pH is too low (under 6), add dolomitic lime; if it's too high (over 7), add elemental sulfur. For additional nitrogen, excellent options are blood meal, mushroom compost, and composted chicken or rabbit manure. Bone meal and rock phosphate add phosphorus, and greensand adds potassium.

What is the difference between slow-release and water-soluble fertilizer? Slow-release fertilizer, available in a dry form, releases its nutrients into the soil over time. This is an excellent addition to the *soil* at the time of planting for long-term fertility. Water-soluble fertilizer such as fish emulsion adds a burst of nutrients and is usually added to the *plants* themselves.

How often should I expect to harvest? Whereas some crops require a daily harvest at their peak (okra, squash), others can be harvested a couple of times per week. But keep in mind that harvesting signals the plants to keep producing. Although there are exceptions (root crops require only one harvest, for example), it's always best to harvest early and often for the highest total yields.

How long through the season should I expect a crop to yield? Crops with a quick-burst harvest such as bush beans, peas, and determinate tomatoes (see tomatoes in part 2) yield over a period of about 3 weeks. Crops with a weather-dependent harvest, such as lettuce, greens, and cilantro, yield until rising temperatures signal the plant to bolt. Under mild conditions, these plants may continue to produce throughout the season. Crops with a full-season harvest, such as pole beans, indeterminate tomatoes, and cucumbers, continue yielding until frost or disease kills them. You can expect to harvest one-and-done crops (for example, garlic) either all at once or over a short period of time, depending on the uniformity of their maturity. Herbs are typically harvested any time, but early in the spring and summer, before flowering, yields the highest quality. Bear in mind that these are generalities, and your climate may affect when and for how long a particular crop yields. Harvest categories are listed in each plant profile in part 2.

PART TWO

Vegetables and Herbs to Grow and Enjoy All Year Round

Now let's take a deeper dive into specific vegetables and herbs. Although this is not an exhaustive list, the more than 30 plants profiled are suitable for first-time gardeners.

This section is meant to be *used*. Use a highlighter and dog-ear pages. Take it into your garden to use the plant-spacing instructions.

Remember, "gardening zones" applies to *perennial* plants, so only the perennial plants list growing zones. To make it easier for you, I've grouped the plants by their growing-climate preference. "Cool-weather" crops generally enjoy growing in the spring and fall, will withstand a frost, and possess varying tolerance to below-freezing temperatures. "Warm-weather" crops will not withstand a frost and must be planted in the garden after the last frost. "Alliums and herbs" include onions, garlic, and annual and perennial herbs. These plants grow a bit differently than the others, which is why they are grouped together. And although some plants (tomatoes, for example) are technically fruits, they're included because they're widely and easily grown at home.

Armed with this section, you might just find yourself grocery shopping from your own garden in a few months!

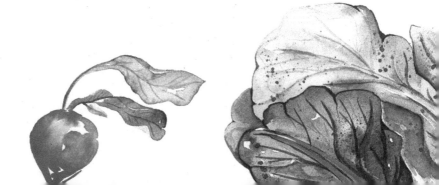

CHAPTER SIX

Cool-Season Vegetables

Arugula
Beets
Broccoli
Brussels Sprouts
Cabbage
Carrots
Green Peas
Kale
Lettuce
Potatoes
Radishes
Spinach
Swiss Chard

Arugula

Family: Brassicaceae

Growing zones: N/A

Growing season(s): cool weather: spring, fall, winter

Spacing: 3 to 6 inches

Start indoors or direct sow: direct sow

Indoor sowing date: N/A

Earliest spring outdoor planting: 6 weeks before average last frost

Soil temperature: 40° to 75°

Fall planting: 2 to 6 weeks before average first frost

Sun needs: 4+ hours

Water needs: low; higher in hot weather

Harvest category: weather dependent

Suggested variety for beginners: N/A

Fun Fact: Though we eat it like lettuce, arugula is actually a member of Brassicaceae, along with broccoli and cabbage. This makes it easy to recognize when the seed germinates, because its sprouts have the distinctive "bow tie" shape.

Snapshot

One of the easiest and most popular greens to grow, arugula thrives in all but
the hottest heat and coldest cold. Its distinctive peppery flavor adds some pep to
salad. You can also enjoy a bowlful of this flavorful green.

Starting

Plant seeds in shallow rows 1 to 2 inches apart, or scatter on top of soil for a bed of
greens. Thin to 3 to 6 inches apart. With a low-growing habit and flexible sunlight
requirements, arugula can be planted at the base of taller crops. Planted densely,
arugula plants will grow smaller but will smother weeds better. Keep the area
moist until germination.

Growing

Since arugula prefers cooler temperatures, mulch after the plants have grown
to about 6 inches tall in order to keep soil temperatures cool. Keep watered in
warm weather.

Harvesting and Storing

Begin picking leaves when they are at least 3 inches long. Harvest from the outside
of the plant first. The leaves taste best when they are picked young; larger leaves
develop a more marked peppery flavor. Store the leaves promptly in a refrigerator
to prevent wilting. Arugula is very cold tolerant, and in many areas you can continue to harvest it throughout the winter.

Common Problem

As temperatures rise in the summer, arugula will begin to bolt in a manner similar
to other greens. Unlike lettuce, bolted arugula leaves aren't inedible, but they will
turn spicy. If you have the space, allow bolted arugula to flower, which will attract
beneficial insects. Left to complete its life cycle, arugula will self-seed, providing
you with another planting and harvest.

Beets

Family: Amaranthaceae

Growing zones: N/A

Growing season(s): cool weather: spring and fall

Spacing: 4 to 6 inches

Start indoors or direct sow: either

Indoor sowing date: 2 to 4 weeks prior to transplant (6 to 8 weeks before average last frost)

Earliest outdoor planting: 4 weeks before average last frost

Soil temperature: 50° to 85°

Fall planting: direct sow, up to 12 weeks before average first frost

Sun needs: 4+ hours

Water needs: moderate

Harvest category: one harvest

Suggested varieties for beginners: Detroit Dark Red, Red Ace, Chioggia, Golden

Preparation Tip: Beets can give you three different harvests. Beet greens 3 inches long are great in salads, so keep them when thinning seedlings. Mature beet greens can be cooked like any other green. And of course, the roots can be harvested early for baby beets or later for full-size beets.

Snapshot

A cool-season root crop that you can grow in rows or tucked into open spaces in your garden, beets can be enjoyed for both the root and the leaves. A loose, sandy loam soil with a near neutral pH (6.5 to 6.8) and ample organic matter offers the best harvest.

Starting

Grown in raised beds, in-ground beds, or containers, beets can be direct sown or started indoors. Each seed actually contains multiple seeds, which you will need to thin to one plant when seedlings get to be 2 to 3 inches tall. If direct sowing, plant these seeds 1 inch apart, ½ inch deep, and thin to a final spacing of 4 to 6 inches apart (if you plant to harvest as baby beets, 2-inch spacing will do). Before sowing, soak seeds for 24 hours in water to speed germination.

Growing

Keep the planting area consistently moist until germination, then keep the area watered regularly. Mulch to conserve moisture, and add a balanced fertilizer or light layer of compost midway through the season.

Harvesting and Storing

If harvesting for both greens and root, you can remove up to one-third of the greens at a time until you are ready to harvest the root. Roots can be harvested at any stage of development. Loosen the soil around the beet with a trowel and pull to harvest. Cut the greens off immediately, leaving about 1 inch of stem if you plan to store them in a root cellar. In climates where the ground doesn't freeze, you can leave a fall planting in the ground and harvest when needed.

Common Problem

Voles (commonly mistaken for mice) hide out in mulch and feast on beet roots. If you have issues with voles, skip the mulch.

Broccoli

Family: Brassicaceae

Growing zones: N/A

Growing season(s): cool weather: spring and fall

Spacing: 18 inches

Start indoors or direct sow: start indoors or purchase transplants

Indoor sowing date: 6 weeks before transplant (9 weeks before average last frost)

Earliest outdoor planting: 3 weeks before average last frost

Soil temperature: N/A

Fall planting: start indoors 12 weeks before average first frost; transplant 6 weeks before average first frost

Sun needs: 6+ hours

Water needs: moderate

Harvest category: one harvest for large head, though some varieties produce side shoots after the head is harvested

Suggested varieties for beginners: Waltham, Packman, Italian Green, Green Comet

Keep in Mind Tip: Broccoli is extremely sensitive to heat, and its tight head will rapidly separate into flowers if temperatures climb in the spring. This is irreversible and signals the end of the plant's growth. To grow broccoli with large heads, start early in the spring (timing is critical for broccoli). Many gardeners find broccoli performs best in the fall, and mature plants are surprisingly cold tolerant.

Snapshot

Broccoli isn't the easiest plant to grow to full maturity, especially in warmer climates, but when you do get to harvest, nothing beats freshly grown stalks.

Starting

Because of its long growth period, broccoli is best started from seed indoors or planted from transplants. With the right timing, indoor sowing is easy, as broccoli seeds germinate rapidly, grow well, and transplant easily. Be sure to pay extra attention to plant timing. When transplanting, allow 12 to 18 inches between plants, because they get large.

Growing

Well-drained, highly fertile soil is key to a healthy plant with a large, harvestable head. Ensure the plants stay well watered throughout their growth.

Harvesting and Storing

Harvest broccoli heads with a sharp knife before the tight clusters begin to separate. Depending on your climate and your season, you may get a larger or smaller head. When the head begins to form in the center of the plant, keep a close eye on it and harvest immediately if the clusters begin to separate. Store in the refrigerator.

Common Problem

Cabbage worms of all types love to feast on broccoli. Use tightly fitting floating row covers immediately upon transplanting to prevent cabbage moths from laying eggs on your broccoli. Otherwise, handpick or use the organic insecticide *Bacillus thuringiensis* at the first sign of damage. Coat both the top and underside of the leaves and reapply after rain.

Brussels Sprouts

CONTAINER-FRIENDLY, RAISED BED–FRIENDLY

Family: Brassicaceae

Growing zones: N/A

Growing season(s): cool weather

Spacing: 18 inches

Start indoors or direct sow: start indoors or purchase transplants

Indoor sowing date: 6 weeks before transplant

Earliest outdoor planting: 3 weeks before average last frost for cold climates; midsummer for warm climates

Soil temperature: N/A

Fall planting: N/A

Sun needs: 6+ hours

Water needs: high

Harvest category: quick burst

Suggested varieties for beginners: Jade Cross Hybrid, Oliver, Long Island Improved

Fun Fact: Grocery-store Brussels sprouts were grown in regions unlikely to have been touched by frost. When you let your mature Brussels sprouts go through a few frosts, you'll taste the difference.

Snapshot

Homegrown Brussels sprouts are much sweeter and more flavorful than their supermarket counterparts. The biggest challenge to growing them is knowing when to plant them. They require a long growing season—three to four months after transplant—but they don't enjoy heat. For cold-weather climates with milder summers, plant in late spring and harvest after frost. For warmer weather climates, delay your planting until mid- to late summer, at least three months prior to your first frost.

Starting

Brussels sprouts can be direct sown into the garden, but opt for transplants if it's your first time growing them, and plant them 18 inches apart. They love a well-drained, sandy loam soil with ample amounts of compost to sustain them throughout the season. Protect them from wind, if possible, by growing them near taller plants, or mound up soil around the stalks to give them a secure base.

Growing

Mulch the plants well to conserve moisture, and keep them watered, particularly in the hot, dry conditions of summer. Because they thrive in rich, fertile soil, Brussels sprouts benefit from supplemental doses of liquid fertilizer such as fish or kelp emulsion a few times throughout the season.

Harvesting and Storing

Harvest Brussels sprouts from the bottom of the stalk to the top when they are about the size of a Ping-Pong ball, before the sprouts start to open. Waiting to harvest them until after a few light frosts sweetens the flavor. Twist the sprouts off and place them in the refrigerator without washing them (water will shorten their storage life).

Common Problem

Because Brussels sprouts grow so slowly, many gardeners wonder if they'll ever get a harvest. Be patient, and if hard frosts begin to arrive, cover the plants with a floating row cover to give them more time. If you still fail to harvest, adjust the timing of your planting next season and focus on high soil fertility at the growing location.

Cabbage

~~~~~~
RAISED BED—FRIENDLY
~~~~~~

Family: Brassicaceae

Growing zones: N/A

Growing season(s): cool weather: spring or fall

Spacing: 18 inches

Start indoors or direct sow: start indoors or purchase transplants

Indoor sowing date: 6 weeks before transplant (9 weeks before average last frost)

Earliest outdoor planting: 3 weeks before average last frost

Soil temperature: N/A

Fall planting: start indoors 12 weeks before average first frost; transplant 6 weeks before average first frost

Sun needs: 6+ hours

Water needs: moderate

Harvest category: one harvest for large head, though some varieties produce small heads after the primary head is harvested

Suggested varieties for beginners: Early Jersey Wakefield, Flat Dutch, Red Acre

Keep in Mind Tip: Because of their long growing season, you may find cabbages still growing in the heat of early summer. Think ahead and plant a vertical crop on the south or west side to provide shade.

Snapshot

Many small-space gardeners skip cabbage because one large plant produces only one head. But for those with a little more space, cabbage is one of the most fun crops to grow, and it provides stunning beauty in the garden.

Starting

Cabbage is best planted as a transplant, whether grown in spring or fall. Start seeds indoors or purchase transplants from a local garden center. Plant transplants a little deeper than they were in their containers, to where the leaves touch the soil level. Cabbage requires a neutral pH soil in a highly fertile location; plant it where other brassicas have not grown for at least the previous three years.

Growing

Cabbage requires consistent moisture, but it doesn't like too much. Mulch well and keep irrigation consistent, especially during dry spells. Add supplemental liquid fertilizer such as fish or kelp emulsion a few times during the growing season if growth seems to lag. Shade plants during times of high heat.

Harvesting and Storing

Harvest cabbage when the heads are large but still firm by cutting the base with a sharp knife. Unless garden space is at a premium, leave the outer leaves; many varieties will produce smaller heads (similar in size to Brussels sprouts). Store in a refrigerator or a root cellar between 33° and 45°.

Common Problem

Cabbage worms prey on cabbage plants of all sizes. Cover transplants with floating row covers immediately upon transplant. Otherwise, handpick worms or spray the organic insecticide *Bacillus thuringiensis* at the first sign of damage.

Carrots

Family: Apiaceae

Growing zones: N/A

Growing season(s): cool weather: spring and fall

Spacing: 2 to 3 inches

Start indoors or direct sow: direct sow

Indoor sowing date: N/A

Earliest outdoor spring planting: 4 to 6 weeks before average last frost

Soil temperature: N/A

Fall planting: 4 to 8 weeks before average first frost

Sun needs: 6+ hours

Water needs: moderate

Harvest category: one harvest

Suggested varieties for beginners: Danvers 126, Scarlet Nantes

Troubleshooting Tip: If you find your harvested carrots bitter in flavor, most likely they matured in hot weather. Replant in the fall for a winter harvest, and you'll find the flavor much sweeter and milder.

Snapshot

Carrots can be some of the most rewarding vegetables to grow, although they can be challenging. Though grown in both the spring and the fall, most gardeners prefer a fall planting, as flavor soars when roots are harvested after several frosts.

Starting

Carrots require loose soil. Prior to planting seeds, use a shovel or trowel to loosen the soil to a depth of about 8 inches. Remove rocks and crush clods. For even rows of carrots, use a rake to create many rows of shallow trenches. Plant the seeds no more than ¼ inch deep, or simply scatter the seeds on top of the soil and graze it with a rake or your fingers to lightly settle the seeds into the soil.

Growing

Carrot seeds can take up to 3 weeks to germinate. Keep the soil evenly moist throughout that time. After seeds germinate, snip extra seedlings at soil level to ensure the final spacing is 2 to 3 inches between plants.

Harvesting and Storing

Plan to begin harvesting around the time when the "days to maturity" on the seed packet has elapsed, though in the fall it may take longer. Use your finger to scrape the dirt around the base of the carrot top, and harvest when the diameter of the root is about 1 inch across (some varieties grow to 2 inches across). To harvest, place a trowel vertically into the soil several inches from the root. Loosen the soil until you can easily pull the carrot. Remove the greens immediately (otherwise the carrots quickly soften), and store the root in the refrigerator. For long-term storage, place the carrots in a container of sand in a cool, dark area such as a garage.

Common Problem

The biggest problem carrot growers face is poor germination. This is usually because the soil was not kept moist. Place a burlap sack or flat floating row cover on top of the soil to limit moisture loss, and supplement with irrigation when rainfall is inadequate.

Green Peas

EXTRA EASY, QUICK, CONTAINER-FRIENDLY, RAISED BED—FRIENDLY, VERTICAL HABIT

Family: Fabaceae

Growing zones: N/A

Growing season(s): cool season: spring and fall

Spacing: 3 inches

Start indoors or direct sow: direct sow

Indoor sowing date: N/A

Earliest outdoor spring planting: as soon as soil can be worked; 6 weeks before average last frost

Soil temperature: 40° to 75° (optimum: 75°)

Fall planting: 4 to 6 weeks before average first frost, snap peas only

Sun needs: 6+ hours daily

Water needs: moderate

Harvest category: quick burst

Suggested varieties for beginners: Green Arrow, Little Marvel, Lincoln, Sugar Snap

Preparation Tip: If you're growing peas for shelling, you will need a lot of room to produce enough to make it worthwhile. A 25-foot row will yield about 1 quart of shelling peas. Snap peas require as little as one-tenth of the space shelling peas require.

Snapshot
Green peas can be grown as snow peas, snap peas, or shelling peas. They prefer cool weather and should be among the first vegetables you plant in the spring. Many varieties require a 3- to 5-foot trellis to support their delicate climbing habit.

Starting
Though you can start pea seeds indoors, they germinate fairly rapidly when sown directly in garden soil. Plant seeds 1 inch deep in a well-draining location; cool, soggy soil can lead to root rot and slow growth. Plant the seeds 1 to 2 inches apart, thinning to a final spacing of 2 to 4 inches apart.

Growing
Because peas are grown in the cool early spring, rainfall is generally sufficient. Place vertical supports in the garden area at planting to avoid disturbing the plant during its growth. Peas prefer horizontal support, such as twine tied between two posts, situated very close to the plants.

Harvesting and Storing
For snow and snap peas, harvest pods before they begin filling with seeds, and for shelling peas, harvest just after the pod swells. Peas are best when picked just before the pods lose their sheen. Refrigerate the pods promptly after picking them, because in heat the natural sugars quickly begin turning to starch.

Common Problem
Peas will stop flowering when air temperatures rise into the upper 80s Fahrenheit. Plan to get your plants into the ground early, in order to harvest them before heat sets in. Powdery mildew can also be a problem, because peas grow during warm days and cool nights, conditions ripe for the disease. Spray the plants with baking soda mixture (see page 68) at the first sign of infection.

Kale

Family: Brassicaceae

Growing zones: N/A

Growing season(s): cool weather: spring, fall, winter

Spacing: 12 to 18 inches

Start indoors or direct sow: either

Indoor sowing date: 6 weeks before transplant (10 weeks before average last frost)

Earliest outdoor planting: 4 to 6 weeks before average last frost

Soil temperature: 45° to 85°

Fall planting: start indoors 12 weeks before average first frost and transplant 6 weeks before average first frost; or direct sow 4 to 6 weeks before average first frost

Sun needs: 6+ hours, can tolerate more shade in the summer

Water needs: moderate

Harvest category: all season in the fall/winter for many areas; weather dependent in spring

Suggested varieties for beginners: Siberian, Tuscan, Red Russian, Winterbor

Fun Fact: One cup of raw kale provides more than 100 percent of the daily recommendations for vitamins A and K.

Snapshot

The poster child for healthy eating, kale can be grown in most gardens at a time when garden space is most available. Kale prefers cold weather, and therefore tastes better when harvested after a frost, making it a prime fall crop. But it can also be planted in the spring and enjoyed before summer crops make their appearance.

Starting

Kale can be started indoors both in the winter (for spring planting) and in the summer (for fall planting) to get a jump-start on the season. It also grows well when sown directly into the garden. Sow seeds 3 inches apart and thin to a final spacing of 12 to 18 inches.

Growing

Kale loves a rich, fertile location with a pH above 5.5 and grows to maturity in about two months. It requires consistent moisture, because its roots are shallow and prone to drying out. Dry roots are especially a concern in the fall, when young plants have grown in a hotter, dryer part of the season. A good layer of mulch will help prevent evaporation, and it will also insulate the soil in the colder parts of the winter, extending the harvest. In most areas, kale will survive the winter; growth will slow or stop in the darkest days, but it will start growing again as daylight increases.

Harvesting and Storing

Like lettuce and other leafy crops, pick young, tender leaves from the outside in. Kale will continue to produce from the inside. Store the leaves in the refrigerator or freezer. Many people find dehydrated "kale chips" a fun treat.

Common Problem

Heat in the summer will toughen the leaves of kale, and often it will bolt in hot weather, sending up flower stalks. To get the most of your harvest, grow kale as a fall crop or plant it in early spring. Then, plan to replace it with a succession planting of a heat-loving plant as the weather warms in the summer.

Lettuce

~~~~~~
EXTRA EASY, QUICK, CONTAINER-FRIENDLY, RAISED BED–FRIENDLY
~~~~~~

Family: Asteraceae

Growing zones: N/A

Growing season(s): cool season: spring and fall

Spacing: leaf lettuce 4 to 6 inches, head lettuce 10 inches

Start indoors or direct sow: either

Indoor sow date: 4 weeks before transplant (8 weeks before average last frost)

Earliest outdoor spring planting: 4 weeks before average last frost, seeds or transplants

Soil temperature: 40° to 80°

Fall planting: 1 to 6 weeks before average first frost

Sun needs: 4+ hours

Water needs: low in spring, more as temperatures climb

Harvest category: weather dependent

Suggested varieties for beginners: Buttercrunch, Cosmo, Parris Island Cos, Rouge d'Hiver

Keep in Mind Tip: Different varieties of lettuce vary in their heat and cold tolerances. Read seed packets to choose heat-tolerant varieties for the spring and cold-tolerant varieties for the fall.

Snapshot

One of the easiest, fastest, and most dependable crops in the home garden, lettuce thrives in the cool temperatures of spring and fall. Some cold-tolerant varieties even survive in the winter, especially when under cover. For a continuous harvest, sow seeds every 2 weeks during the spring and fall.

Starting

Lettuce can be started from seed indoors for a jump start to the spring harvest or for a fall crop when the late summer is too hot for lettuce to thrive. Whether starting indoors or direct sowing, scatter seeds on top of the soil and gently graze it with your fingers or a rake to lightly settle the seeds into the soil. Don't bury the seeds, as a surface sowing will result in the best germination. Keep the area moist. Thin seedlings to desired spacing.

Growing

Once established, lettuce requires little maintenance. Ensure the area stays watered, and watch out for insects such as aphids and worms. Lettuce is a great crop to plant under vertical crops such as tomatoes, peas, and beans. The vertical crops will provide shade for the lettuce, possibly allowing a longer harvest time into the summer. Mulch well to keep soil temperatures low, which may delay bolting.

Harvesting and Storing

Harvest the outermost leaves of leaf lettuce. The plants will continue to produce from the center. Keep an eye on early summer weather, because warm temperatures and dry conditions will cause the plant to bolt and the leaves to turn bitter. For head lettuce (usually only successful in cooler climates), harvest when heads are firm.

Common Problem

When lettuce begins to form a stalk in the center, it has reached the end of its life cycle (also known as bolting). At this point, the leaves are bitter beyond edibility and you can't do anything to change it. If space is at a premium, pull the plants and compost them, but if not, allow the plants to form flower stalks, which will attract beneficial insects.

Potatoes

Family: Solanaceae

Growing zones: N/A

Growing season(s): cool weather: spring

Spacing: 12 inches

Start indoors or direct sow: direct sow "seed" potatoes

Indoor sowing date: N/A

Earliest outdoor planting: 4 to 6 weeks before average last frost

Soil temperature: 50° to 80°

Fall planting: 12 to 14 weeks before average first frost

Sun needs: 6+ hours

Water needs: moderate

Harvest category: one harvest

Suggested varieties for beginners: Red Norland, Yukon Gold, Kennebec

Troubleshooting Tip: Although potato leaves are frost tolerant, they will die in a hard freeze. If a freeze is imminent and stems have already emerged, cover the plants with a light temporary mulch or cover. If leaves experience freeze damage, clip affected leaves off; often the plant will rebound with new growth.

Snapshot

Potatoes can be one of the most fun vegetables to grow and harvest. In cold-season areas, the plants grow all season for a late-summer harvest. In warm-season areas, tubers are harvested in early summer, leaving space for a succession crop. Some varieties (such as red potatoes) harvest as early as 60 days from planting; other varieties (such as White Russet) may take four months.

Starting

Purchase "seed" potatoes from a local farmers' co-op, a feed store, or a reputable online seed supplier. These are small potatoes produced in a certified disease-free environment. When the soil is able to be worked in the spring, dig trenches 4 inches deep with a hoe, and set the seed potatoes in the trenches 12 inches apart. Return the soil to the trench, covering the seed potatoes completely, and mark your rows. Depending on the weather and soil temperature, look for tough, dark green, rosette-like stems to emerge in about 3 weeks.

Growing

When plants are about 6 inches tall, take a hoe and pull the surrounding soil up to make "hills" around the plants. Repeat this process about 3 weeks later. Potato tubers begin growing at soil level, but if exposed to light, they develop green skin, which is toxic in large amounts. "Hilling" provides space for tubers to grow without sunlight. Keep the ground evenly watered but not saturated.

Harvesting and Storing

Watch for the vines to begin losing their deep green color and vigor. This is called "dying back." Wait about 3 weeks. Then take a shovel and dig about 12 inches away from the main plant, loosening the soil around it. Tubers should be most evident right at soil level. Be careful handling the tubers because they bruise easily. At harvest they are ready to eat, but if you want to store them longer, place unwashed tubers in a cool, dark location for 1 or 2 weeks before moving them to the coolest spot in your home or a root cellar (50° is ideal).

Common Problem

Early blight, which affects tomatoes, also causes yellowing spots on potato leaves. Do not plant potatoes where tomatoes have grown in the past three to four years. Mulch using organic hay or straw.

Radishes

Family: Brassicaceae

Growing zones: N/A

Growing season(s): cool weather: spring and fall

Spacing: 2 to 4 inches

Start indoors or direct sow: direct sow

Indoor sowing date: N/A

Earliest outdoor planting: 6 weeks before average last frost

Soil temperature: 45° to 90°

Fall planting: 4 weeks before average first frost

Sun needs: 4+ hours

Water needs: low

Harvest category: one harvest

Suggested varieties for beginners: Cherry Belle, French Breakfast, Icicle

Fun Fact: Plant radish and carrot seeds in the same row. Quick-germinating radish seeds help mark the row where slow-germinating carrot seeds eventually sprout. Radishes will be ready to harvest before carrots need the space.

Snapshot

One of the quickest, easiest garden vegetables to grow, radishes are usually among the first to harvest in the spring. They require little space and can be easily tucked into vacant soil in containers, raised beds, and in-ground gardens.

Starting

Radishes don't require any special soil. Scatter seeds or sow them in rows, but don't spread them too thickly, because they usually germinate quite well. For multiple harvests, schedule succession plantings 10 days apart up until about a month before hot weather sets in.

Growing

Radishes usually grow well on their own without much intervention. Thin extra sprouts to 1 to 2 inches apart and mulch to prevent weeds. Watch for the radish roots to begin poking out of the soil, signaling they're ready to harvest.

Harvesting and Storing

Begin harvesting when the tops of the radishes start to emerge from the soil, usually when they're about 1 inch in diameter. Don't leave them in the ground too long; the longer they stay in the soil, the tougher they'll get. You can leave a few in the ground to bolt and flower. Beneficial insects love these flowers, and left to go to seed, radishes can self-sow for another crop.

Common Problem

When radishes are grown in the heat of the summer (or when you delay harvest for too long), the taste becomes sharp, pungent, and sometimes bitter or spicy. For a sweeter flavor, harvest before hot weather sets in.

Spinach

CONTAINER-FRIENDLY, RAISED BED—FRIENDLY

Family: Amaranthaceae

Growing zones: N/A

Growing season(s): cool weather: spring, fall, winter

Spacing: 4 to 6 inches

Start indoors or direct sow: either

Indoor sowing date: 4 weeks before transplant (10 weeks before average last frost in spring or 4 to 8 weeks before last frost in fall)

Earliest outdoor spring planting: 6 weeks before average last frost

Soil temperature: 45° to 75°

Fall planting: 6 weeks before average first frost (direct sow), 0 to 6 weeks before average first frost (transplant)

Sun needs: 4+ hours

Water needs: moderate

Harvest category: weather dependent

Suggested varieties for beginners: Bloomsdale Long Standing, Indian Summer, Olympia

Keep in Mind Tip: Because spinach loves the cooler weather, it is an excellent succession plant. One garden idea is to interplant young peppers with spinach one month after the last-frost date. After the spinach bolts, pull it out to give the peppers room to expand in the heat. In the fall, plant spinach seeds beneath the shade of peppers for a second planting.

100 VEGETABLE GARDENING FOR BEGINNERS

Snapshot

One of the most nutritious greens you can eat, spinach can be one of the most dependable, hardy greens to grow. It's a bit more difficult to germinate than other greens, but when established, it's a pretty hands-off crop.

Starting

Most gardeners start growing spinach in the spring, and the earlier the better. But an even better time of year to start growing it is in the fall and winter, since it loves cold weather. Direct sow spinach seeds ¼ inch deep in a shallow furrow, cover with soil, and water well. If you start the seeds indoors, choose a deep container, because spinach develops a taproot, and take special care when transplanting.

Growing

Mulch spinach plants well to regulate soil temperature in both the summer and the winter. In the winter, the plants enjoy the full sun of the shorter days, but in the spring and summer, they benefit from shade cast by larger plants. In the winter, as the length of the day dips below 10 hours, spinach will stop growing. But you can still harvest up to one-third of the leaves. A few weeks later, if new leaves have formed, you can harvest another one-third. When days begin to lengthen in the spring, spinach will resume its growth in all but the coldest regions.

Harvesting and Storing

Harvest the outer leaves first, either as small leaves for baby spinach or larger leaves for spinach greens. Store the leaves in the refrigerator promptly after harvest.

Common Problem

As days lengthen and heat sets in, spinach will bolt and send up a flower stalk. When this happens, check the taste of the leaves; often they become bitter. If you have the space, leave bolted plants to flower and attract beneficial insects.

Swiss Chard

EXTRA EASY, QUICK, CONTAINER-FRIENDLY, RAISED BED—FRIENDLY

Family: Amaranthaceae

Growing zones: N/A

Growing season(s): cool weather: spring and fall

Spacing: 6 to 12 inches

Start indoors or direct sow: direct sow

Indoor sowing date: N/A

Earliest outdoor planting: 4 weeks before last frost

Soil temperature: 50° to 85°

Fall planting: 10 weeks before average first frost

Sun needs: 4+ hours

Water needs: moderate

Harvest category: all season, occasionally weather dependent

Suggested varieties for beginners: Fordhook Giant, Bright Lights, Rhubarb Supreme

Preparation Tip: Young leaves can be used in salads. Both mature stems and leaves can be used in stir-fries; just cook the stems longer and add the leaves toward the end.

Snapshot

Swiss chard is a highly nutritious plant and a gorgeous addition to any garden. Less likely to bolt in hot weather than other greens and highly tolerant of cold, this leafy relative of beets and spinach can be enjoyed in multiple seasons.

Starting

Swiss chard isn't demanding when it comes to soil, although it enjoys a slightly acidic pH (6.0 to 7.0) and thrives in a well-draining, loamy location. Direct sow seeds, spacing them 1 to 2 inches apart. As the seedlings emerge, cut extra seedlings at the soil line (save them for microgreens!) to a final spacing of 6 to 12 inches apart.

Growing

If Swiss chard bolts at all, it will not bolt in hot weather as quickly as other greens. Mulching around the plants will moderate soil moisture and temperature, preventing the plant from bolting. Keep the watering consistent, because lack of water may be a bigger factor than temperature in premature bolting.

Harvesting and Storing

Harvest young greens at 4 inches long, working from the outside in. For a harvest of both stems and leaves, harvest the entire plant when the largest leaves are 10 inches long, cutting about 2 inches above the soil surface. Leave the plant to resprout. Refrigerate the leaves and stalks and wash them only prior to cooking or eating them.

Common Problem

Slugs and snails love Swiss chard, especially in cooler, wetter times of the year. Spread a thin line of diatomaceous earth on the soil around each plant, and hand-pick any pests you spot on the leaves.

CHAPTER SEVEN

Warm-Season Vegetables

Corn
Cucumber
Eggplant
Green Beans
Melons
Okra
Peppers
Pumpkins and Winter Squash
Summer Squash and Zucchini
Sweet Potatoes
Tomatoes

Corn

Family: Poaceae

Growing zones: N/A

Growing season(s): warm weather

Spacing: 12 inches

Start indoors or direct sow: direct sow

Indoor sowing date: N/A

Earliest outdoor planting: after last frost

Soil temperature: 60° to 95°

Fall planting: 14 weeks before average first frost

Sun needs: 8+ hours

Water needs: high

Harvest category: one harvest

Suggested varieties for beginners: Golden Bantam, Jubilee, Peaches and Cream, Silver Queen

Fun Fact: Legend says that Native Americans placed a fish in the planting hole before planting corn. Considering corn's high nitrogen requirements, this method has some merit. They also planted pole beans and squash around corn—known as the "three sisters" technique—a type of companion planting that many people still use today.

Snapshot

Nothing beats a bite of freshly picked corn on the cob in the height of summer. As long as you plant enough for proper pollination and provide ample nitrogen and water, you can enjoy one of summer's best treats.

Starting

Plant corn seeds every 3 inches, 1 inch deep. Thin seedlings to a final spacing of 12 inches. Make sure the soil has been enriched with compost or another high-nitrogen amendment such as composted manure. Because corn is wind-pollinated and each kernel requires one grain of pollen, plant at least four rows of four plants each—the more the better.

Growing

Set drip irrigation at the base of the rows to ensure the corn gets enough water during the growing season. Besides its need for water, corn grows fairly easily on its own. For smaller plantings where pollination might be a concern, shake the cornstalks when you see silky strands emerging from the corn's ears. Pollen from the tassels at the top of the plant will blow and drop on the silks.

Harvesting and Storing

Watch for the silks of the corn to turn brown and completely dry out. When the silk sloughs off the plant with the slightest touch, it's ready to harvest. To test it, pull down part of the corn's husk until you see the filled-out kernels a couple of inches from the tip of the ear. Prick a kernel with your fingernail. If the substance is milky-white, it's ready; if it's clear, give it a few more days. If no fluid comes out, sadly, it's too late. Snap the ears off with a brisk twisting motion. Serve as soon as possible, because up to 50 percent of the sugars in corn convert to starch in the first 24 hours after harvest.

Common Problem

Corn earworms burrow undetected into the tips of the developing ear. Snap off the damaged portion and dispose of the worm; the rest of the corn cob is fine to eat. Some gardeners find success applying mineral oil to the silks about 5 days after the silks first appear.

Cucumber

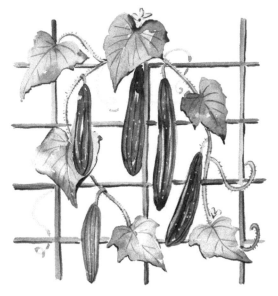

~~~~~~
EXTRA EASY, CONTAINER-FRIENDLY, RAISED BED—FRIENDLY, VERTICAL HABIT
~~~~~~

Family: Cucurbitaceae

Growing zones: N/A

Growing season(s): warm weather

Spacing: 9 inches

Start indoors or direct sow: direct sow

Indoor sowing date: N/A

Earliest outdoor planting: after last frost

Soil temperature: 60° to 95°

Fall planting: 12+ weeks before average first frost

Sun needs: 8+ hours

Water needs: high

Harvest category: all season

Suggested varieties for beginners: Marketmore 76, Chicago Pickling, Bush Pickle

Troubleshooting Tip: Uneven watering can cause bitter cucumbers. To curb the bite, cut off the blossom end of the fruit and rub the two pieces together until a foam appears. Wash the foam away. Then peel the cucumber; much of the bitterness is contained in the skin. Ensure the remaining plant stays on a consistent watering schedule to prevent bitter cucumbers in the future.

Snapshot

This versatile summer staple finds its way into many gardens. Most varieties climb a vertical trellis, making it an excellent candidate for companion planting, but some bush types sport a compact habit suitable for containers. Choose pickling varieties if you want to make pickles because their skin absorbs the brine easily. Choose a burpless slicing variety for fresh eating.

Starting

Because cucumbers do not transplant easily, direct sow the seeds once soil temperatures warm. Keep the soil moist but not soggy; soggy soil can cause the seed to rot. Sow seeds 1 inch deep every 3 inches, thinning to a final spacing of 6 to 9 inches for vining types and 12 inches for bush types. Ensure the soil contains rich organic matter such as compost.

Growing

Keep cucumbers evenly watered throughout the growing season but especially when they're flowering. Use a drip system or soaker hose to prevent common diseases such as powdery mildew or downy mildew. Train climbing varieties up their structure by weaving the stems through the support. Tendrils latch on to both vertical and horizontal structures, making a fence or weave pattern ideal.

Harvesting and Storing

Harvest pickling cucumbers when they reach 3 to 4 inches long. Pick slicing varieties at 6 to 8 inches long. If any grow too large, cut them off anyway, otherwise the plant will slow production. Store the cucumbers in a refrigerator; if pickling, try to use freshly picked cucumbers as soon as possible.

Common Problem

Powdery mildew and downy mildew can stunt the growth of and eventually kill the cucumber plant. Spray leaves with a baking soda mixture (see page 68) at the first sign of either mildew. Sudden wilting of the plant can be caused by bacterial wilt, transmitted by cucumber beetles. Destroy the plant; it cannot be saved.

Eggplant

Family: Solanaceae

Growing zones: N/A

Growing season(s): warm weather

Spacing: 18 to 24 inches

Start indoors or direct sow: start indoors or purchase transplants

Earliest outdoor planting: 2 weeks after last spring frost

Soil temperature: 75° to 90°

Indoor sowing date: 8 to 12 weeks before transplant (6 to 10 weeks before average last frost)

Fall planting: 16 weeks before average first frost (for warmer climates only)

Sun needs: 8+ hours

Water needs: moderate

Harvest category: all season

Suggested varieties for beginners: Black Beauty, Dusky, Orient Express, Easter Egg

Preparation Tip: If frost threatens and your eggplants only have small fruit, pick them for a delicious side dish of baby eggplant.

Snapshot

Heat is the name of the game in growing eggplant. It thrives in southern gardens, but northern gardeners can enjoy this gorgeous vegetable with a few extra measures. If you live in an area with shorter summers, get a head start by starting seeds indoors, and plant them in raised beds or containers where soil warms up quickly.

Starting

If you're starting seeds indoors, ensure the soil is warm. Use a seedling heat mat (helpful with peppers, too), or place the seed tray on a clothes dryer or refrigerator. Transfer growing seedlings to larger pots as necessary until the weather has stabilized and is consistently warm outside for transplant. When hardened off, plant eggplants 18 to 24 inches apart.

Growing

Although not required, eggplants can benefit from trellising to keep fruit off the ground. A simple tomato cage works well. Keep the ground evenly watered and mulch well, because the eggplant's root system is shallow. Avoid using a hoe to weed around the plant, as this could damage the root system.

Harvesting and Storing

Eggplants, unlike other fruiting vegetables, can be picked at various sizes. Young eggplants can be harvested at one-third of their mature size; just make sure to harvest them when the skin is still shiny. Cut the fruits off at the stem; don't yank or twist them because this could damage the plant. Store eggplants in the refrigerator or in a location at 40° to 50°, which is ideal.

Common Problem

Flea beetles are typically the eggplant's worst pest, preying especially on young plants. Cover transplants with a floating row cover and remove it when flowering begins.

Green Beans

Family: Fabaceae

Growing zones: N/A

Growing season(s): warm weather

Spacing: 6 inches

Start indoors or direct sow:
direct sow

Indoor sowing date: N/A

Earliest outdoor planting: after
last frost

Soil temperature: 60° to 85°

Fall planting: bush beans only,
75 days before average first frost

Sun needs: 8+ hours

Water needs: moderate

Harvest category: quick burst
(bush), full season (pole)

Suggested varieties for beginners:
Blue Lake, Kentucky Wonder,
Contender

Keep in Mind Tip: Although beans can be grown in containers, you may not have the space to grow enough to make it worth it. Plant a minimum of 5 to 10 plants for a couple of fresh meals.

Snapshot

Beautiful, prolific, and easily harvested, green beans are among the first plants beginning gardeners grow. The only real decision you'll need to make is whether to grow bush beans or pole beans. Bush beans harvest earlier, do not need a trellis, and produce within a 2- to 3-week span. Pole beans start bearing later, require a trellis, bear until killed by frost, and produce a greater total yield. Bush beans are a great succession crop, but pole beans require less ground space, allowing more plants to be grown in a limited area.

Starting

Wait until the soil has warmed before planting bean seeds. Although some germination will occur at 60°, the warmer the soil, the higher the germination rate will be. Plant seeds 3 inches apart, 1 inch deep in a full-sun location. After germination, thin plants as necessary to 6 inches apart. Avoid planting in wet, soggy soil because the seeds may rot before germination begins.

Growing

Beans require little maintenance during the growing season. Just ensure pole beans have a trellis to climb. Keep developing plants well watered, and watch for insect damage.

Harvesting and Storing

Snap beans are ready to harvest at about 4 inches long, depending on the variety. Pods should snap easily when bent, but the seeds inside should not be large enough to bulge in the pod. Perfect pods still have a sheen on the outside. For pole beans, pick regularly, because picking signals the plant to keep producing. Store freshly picked green beans in the refrigerator.

Common Problem

Beetles are the biggest problem for green beans. Plant as early as the soil temperature allows to get a head start on growth. Mature bean plants withstand insect damage better than young ones. Handpick beetles you see. For heavy infestations, look at organic repellent options such as kaolin clay or neem oil.

Melons

~~~~~~
CONTAINER-FRIENDLY, RAISED BED–FRIENDLY, VERTICAL HABIT
~~~~~~

Family: Cucurbitaceae

Growing zones: N/A

Growing season(s): warm weather

Spacing: 18 inches if growing vertically; 2 to 3 feet if not

Start indoors or direct sow: direct sow

Indoor sowing date: N/A

Earliest outdoor planting: after last frost

Soil temperature: 70° to 95°

Fall planting: N/A

Sun needs: 8+ hours

Water needs: high

Harvest category: all season

Suggested varieties for beginners: Watermelon: Crimson Sweet, Sugar Baby, Charleston Grey, Georgia Rattlesnake. Cantaloupe: Ambrosia, Hale's Best. Honeydew: Earli-Dew

Fun Fact: Watermelon contains more lycopene than tomatoes. Lycopene has been shown to reduce risk for certain types of cancer and heart attack, making watermelon not only a delicious summertime treat but also a healthy one.

Snapshot

Growing on sprawling vines, melons require a lot of space. If space is limited, grow small-fruited varieties in raised beds or containers, making sure to set up a trellis for them. Plant seeds as soon as possible in the spring, as melons do best with a long, hot growing season.

Starting

Sow seeds 1 inch deep, 6 inches apart, then thin seedlings to final spacing. Don't plant the seeds in cool, wet soil or they will not germinate. Amend the planting area with compost, and mulch seedlings to conserve moisture.

Growing

Use drip irrigation to keep melons well watered throughout the season. If you're growing melons vertically, train the vines as they grow; support developing fruits with hammocks made of old T-shirts. After three to five fruits have developed on one vine, cut the tip off the vine to encourage the vine to ripen the fruit already present instead of producing more fruit.

Harvesting and Storing

Cantaloupe and honeydew change color and slip off the vine with a gentle tug. The skin of watermelons will start to turn from shiny to dull as ripening nears. Look for a tendril nearest the stem of the watermelon. When that tendril has completely dried to brown, shut off irrigation and wait about 1 week. Then harvest. Time your harvest during a dry spell if possible, because this will concentrate the sugars in the fruit.

Common Problem

Deformed fruit can be caused by a lack of pollination. Sometimes bees haven't found your melon flowers yet; just give it time. But if this continues to be an issue, consider hand-pollinating (see pages 68–69). Blossom-end rot is also common in melons. Keep moisture consistent to prevent this condition. Remove deformed fruit to signal the plant to produce more.

Okra

Family: Malvaceae

Growing zones: N/A

Growing season(s): warm weather

Spacing: 12 to 24 inches

Start indoors or direct sow: direct sow, except in cooler climates

Indoor sowing date: 4 weeks before transplant (2 weeks before last frost)

Earliest outdoor planting: 2 to 4 weeks after last frost

Soil temperature: 70° to 95°

Fall planting: N/A

Sun needs: 8+ hours

Water needs: low

Harvest category: all season

Suggested varieties for beginners: Clemson Spineless, Red Burgundy, Annie Oakley II, Cajun Delight

Preparation Tip: Though okra lovers praise a good southern-fried okra side dish, okra is also delicious roasted. Toss whole pods in olive oil and sprinkle them with sea salt, pepper, and garlic powder. Bake in a 400° oven for 20 minutes.

Snapshot

Okra is originally from Africa but has become a staple in the southern garden and in southern cooking. Although this gorgeous plant with showy flowers thrives in long, hot summers, many northern gardeners can grow okra with a few adjustments.

Starting

Okra is best sown directly in the garden. For faster germination, soak seeds overnight and plant in warm soil. Okra can be grown in raised beds that open up to the ground. Its long taproot needs the depth to grow into the native soil. (Grow compact varieties in containers 24 inches deep.) Sow seeds ½ inch deep, 6 inches apart. Thin seedlings to a final spacing of 12 to 24 inches. If you start the seeds early indoors, plant them in a deep container to accommodate the developing taproot.

Growing

Okra will grow slowly in the early summer but then quicken its growth when daytime temperatures reach the 80s or 90s Fahrenheit, and even higher. Once established, okra is a self-sufficient crop. It tolerates drought but also likes a regular weekly watering.

Harvesting and Storing

Cut okra pods with pruners when they reach 4 to 5 inches long (some varieties must be cut smaller). Any longer than this and you'll find them tough and woody (and inedible). During peak season, harvest at least daily (sometimes twice per day). Store the pods in the refrigerator. If you skip a day and the pods grow too big, pick them anyway and compost them, otherwise the plant will slow production.

Common Problem

Okra doesn't fall prey to many pests or diseases. When other plants suffer during hot weather, okra shines. One problem many gardeners have is a skin sensitivity to the plant leaves. Wear gloves when harvesting.

Peppers

EXTRA EASY, CONTAINER-FRIENDLY, RAISED BED—FRIENDLY

Family: Solanaceae

Growing zones: N/A

Growing season(s): warm weather

Spacing: 18 inches

Start indoors or direct sow: start indoors or purchase transplants

Indoor sowing date: 8 weeks before transplant (6 weeks before average last frost)

Earliest outdoor planting: 2 weeks after last spring frost

Soil temperature: 65° to 95°

Fall planting: N/A

Sun needs: 8+ hours

Water needs: high

Harvest category: all season

Suggested varieties for beginners: California Wonder, Emerald Giant, jalapeño, poblano, Anaheim, cayenne

Preparation Tip: If you harvest more bell peppers than you can use fresh, slice or chop them, lay them on a rimmed baking sheet in a single layer, and freeze them. Once they're frozen, scoop the peppers into resealable freezer bags for storing and use them year-round.

Snapshot

An iconic summer vegetable, peppers make an appearance in almost every garden. Whether you grow bell, hot, specialty, or a combination, give peppers warm weather, plenty of water, and ample soil fertility, and enjoy this versatile vegetable until frost. Peppers are actually a perennial vegetable, so if your area doesn't receive frosts, you may enjoy peppers year-round.

Starting

Start seeds indoors in a soil warmed with a seedling heat mat or placed on top of a clothes dryer or refrigerator. Seeds can take a couple of weeks to sprout. Transfer them to larger pots as the plants grow, and don't plant them in the garden too early. Peppers thrive in hot weather; wait until nighttime temperatures are consistently in the upper 50s Fahrenheit at minimum. Peppers grow well in raised beds and containers, where the soil heats up faster.

Growing

Young peppers benefit from fish emulsion applied every couple of weeks until flowering. Then switch to a phosphorus-rich fertilizer such as liquid kelp. Stake plants by tying the main stem to a wooden stake, or use a tomato cage. Keep in full sun, though growers in southern areas with oppressive summer heat may find afternoon shade beneficial.

Harvesting and Storing

Bell peppers can be harvested green or left on the plant to ripen into their mature color (usually red but also yellow, purple, or brown). Pick green peppers early for highest production, because this signals the plant to keep flowering and fruiting. Toward the middle of the season, start letting peppers ripen to their mature color. As the days get shorter, this ripening process quickens. Store peppers in the refrigerator.

Common Problem

Dark, rotten areas on fruit are either caused by blossom-end rot or piercing insect damage. In the case of blossom-end rot, ensure plants are evenly watered and mulched. The rest of the fruit is edible; just cut around the blemish. White areas on the fruit are caused by sunscald (too much sun exposure to the fruit itself). Provide afternoon shade until the hottest weather passes.

Pumpkins and Winter Squash

~~~
CONTAINER-FRIENDLY, RAISED BED—FRIENDLY, VERTICAL HABIT
~~~

Family: Cucurbitaceae

Growing zones: N/A

Growing season(s): warm weather

Spacing: 24 inches if growing vertically; 4 to 6 feet if not

Start indoors or direct sow: direct sow

Indoor sowing date: N/A

Earliest outdoor planting: after last frost

Soil temperature: 70° to 90°

Fall planting: N/A

Sun needs: 8+ hours

Water needs: high

Harvest category: varies by type, but mostly quick harvest

Suggested varieties for beginners: Buttercup, Early Butternut, Waltham, Vegetable Spaghetti, Connecticut Field (large pumpkin), Seminole (pie pumpkin)

Preparation Tip: If you want to grow pumpkins for pies or breads, choose a variety specifically labeled "pie pumpkin". Large pumpkins for carving are not ideal for baking.

Snapshot

Contrary to its name, winter squash (and pumpkin) grows during the summer. It matures in the fall, and because of its ability to be stored for a long time is usually consumed in the winter, hence its designation.

Starting

Winter squash and pumpkins require a long growing season, and fertile soil rich in organic matter is essential. These seeds are best sown directly in warm soil. In colder climates they may benefit from being started indoors, while black plastic covers and warms the soil ahead of planting. You can also plant winter squash and pumpkin seeds in the warmer soil of raised beds or containers. Sow the seeds 6 inches apart, then thin to 2 feet apart (for compact varieties or those growing up a trellis) or 4 to 6 feet apart.

Growing

Consistent watering is key to properly developed pumpkins and winter squash. If you're growing them on a trellis, train the vines by weaving them around the vertical support. Use old T-shirts fashioned into hammocks to support developing fruits. Larger pumpkin varieties should not be grown vertically because they get too heavy.

Harvesting and Storing

Harvest winter squash and pumpkins before the first frost. Look for the skins to change to a dull color and the stem to become woody. Also, use your fingernail to try to indent the rind. If no mark remains, the squash or pumpkin is ready to pick. When you cut off the gourd, leave 2 inches of the stem intact. Store your crops in a hot area (85° to 90°) for several days before moving them into cold storage at 50° to 60°.

Common Problem

Squash vine borers commonly affect pumpkins and winter squash in some parts of the country. If leaves wilt overnight, inspect the base of the plant for sawdust-like frass. Slice the stem open with a knife and look for a white grub (sometimes there are several). Dispose of the grub and bury the injured stem so it can grow new roots. Water well.

Summer Squash and Zucchini

~~~
QUICK, CONTAINER-FRIENDLY, RAISED BED–FRIENDLY
~~~

Family: Cucurbitaceae

Growing zones: N/A

Growing season(s): warm weather

Spacing: 24 to 36 inches

Start indoors or direct sow: direct sow

Indoor sowing date: N/A

Earliest outdoor planting: after last frost

Soil temperature: 70° to 95°

Fall planting: 12 weeks before average first frost

Sun needs: 8+ hours

Water needs: high

Harvest category: all season

Suggested varieties for beginners: Yellow Crookneck, Black Beauty, White Scallop

Troubleshooting Tip: If squash vine borers kill your early squash planting, sow seeds again for an early fall planting. In many areas, this midsummer sowing will skip the life cycle of the squash vine borer, giving you a bumper crop headed into fall.

Snapshot

Many gardeners experience summer squash and zucchini as a feast-or-famine crop. Some years we're dropping off bags of squash on our neighbors' doorsteps, and other years we're lucky to get a handful. Squash vine borers, squash bugs, powdery mildew, downy mildew, and lack of pollination can frustrate a gardener, but because squash is a quick-growing crop, there's usually a way to grow multiple plantings if these issues do arise.

Starting

Direct sow when the soil has warmed in the spring, after the danger of frost has passed. Sow 1 inch deep every 3 to 6 inches and thin to 2 to 4 feet apart. Don't overcrowd these plants, otherwise they will compete for nutrients and water, and the yield will suffer. Give them plenty of room and lots of organic matter, such as compost, at planting time.

Growing

Keep squash plants consistently irrigated, especially at the time of flowering and fruiting. Cut yellowed, dead stems off as the plant grows, to increase circulation and curtail disease. Watch for early signs of pests and disease.

Harvesting and Storing

Once you see a baby squash or zucchini, prepare to harvest within a few days, because this fruit grows fast. Harvest the fruit when it is small, for the best taste and texture when eating it fresh. Plan to use any larger squash or zucchini you may have missed in breads. Take a sharp knife to harvest at the stem to prevent damage to the plant.

Common Problem

If you notice the baby fruit not growing and eventually rotting, most likely the fruit was never pollinated. In the absence of pollinators, be prepared to hand-pollinate (see pages 68–69). Often, you'll only have to do this for a short time until the pollinators arrive.

Sweet Potatoes

CONTAINER-FRIENDLY, RAISED BED–FRIENDLY

Family: Convolvulaceae

Growing zones: N/A

Growing season(s): warm weather

Spacing: 12 to 18 inches

Start indoors or direct sow: direct sow "slips"

Indoor sowing date: N/A

Earliest outdoor planting: 2 weeks after last frost

Soil temperature: 65°+

Fall planting: N/A

Sun needs: 8+ hours

Water needs: high

Harvest category: one harvest

Suggested varieties for beginners: Beauregard, Georgia Jet, Centennial

Fun Fact: Considered a "superfood" by many people, antioxidant-rich sweet potatoes boast high levels of fiber, beta carotene, vitamin A, vitamin C, and potassium. Contrary to popular belief, sweet potatoes and yams are completely different vegetables.

Snapshot
Sweet potatoes require a long, hot growing season. If you live in a shorter-season area, choose a variety with fewer days to maturity. They also need space to sprawl, but this can be achieved by simply letting the vines spill out of your container or raised bed. Wherever you grow them, ensure the sweet potatoes have plenty of water and well-draining soil.

Starting
Purchase certified disease-free "slips" (baby plants) from a local garden center or reputable online supplier. Plant them 12 to 18 inches apart when the weather is consistently warm (80s Fahrenheit is ideal). Should a late frost threaten, plan to cover the young vines.

Growing
Provide consistent water and do not add additional nitrogen fertilizer. Sweet potatoes grow best in slightly acidic, sandy loam soil with good amounts of phosphorus and potassium. Rock phosphate and greensand are good soil amendments for sweet potato beds.

Harvesting and Storing
Dig up sweet potatoes after the vines start to turn yellow, or prior to your first frost. Dig carefully, as tubers can grow several feet away from the main plant. Young sweet potatoes can suffer damage easily, so handle them gently. Transfer them, unwashed, to a hot area (85° to 95°) with high humidity for 7 to 10 days. Then place them in cool storage at 50° to 60°. Use damaged tubers immediately after curing.

Common Problem
Tubers can suffer rot if planted in an area that doesn't drain well. Site your location carefully, and if you're planting a smaller crop, choose raised beds or containers to ensure proper drainage.

Tomatoes

Family: Solanaceae

Growing zones: N/A

Growing season(s): warm weather

Spacing: 24 to 36 inches

Start indoors or direct sow: start indoors or purchase transplants

Indoor sowing date: 6 weeks before average last frost

Earliest outdoor planting: after last frost

Soil temperature: 60° to 85°

Fall planting: N/A

Sun needs: 6+ hours

Water needs: moderate

Harvest category: quick burst (determinate varieties); all season (indeterminate varieties)

Suggested varieties for beginners: Roma, Sungold, Better Boy, Juliet

Troubleshooting Tip: Early blight is the most common issue for tomatoes, especially during rainy periods. Mulch the soil heavily. Remove affected yellowing stems immediately and dispose of them to prevent the spread of the blight.

Snapshot

The most commonly grown vegetable in an edible garden, tomatoes come in all sizes, flavors, and growth habits. Smaller-fruited varieties such as cherry and paste tomatoes may prove easiest for a beginner, but with proper care the larger slicing types grace the plates of many first-time gardeners. **Determinate tomatoes** are varieties that grow to a specific size (usually 3 to 5 feet) and set all their fruit in a 2- to 4-week window. After this period, they set little if any fruit. The Roma tomato is a common determinate variety. **Indeterminate tomatoes** are varieties that continue to grow and set fruit until they are killed by frost or disease. Most tomatoes are indeterminate, including popular slicing varieties.

Starting

Tomatoes grow best when planted outside after nighttime temperatures rise consistently into the 50s Fahrenheit. This necessitates starting seeds indoors or purchasing transplants. When planting transplants, bury the stem up to where the top leaves rise only a few inches above soil level. (Tomato stems will produce roots along any buried stem.) Choose and install your staking or caging method at planting time.

Growing

Water at soil level to prevent common soilborne diseases from splashing onto plants. Drip irrigation or soaker hoses keep water consistent, preventing most cases of blossom-end rot. As the plant grows, situate vines to grow up the trellis, or tie vines to a stake.

Harvesting and Storing

Harvest tomatoes as soon as the bottom of the fruit begins to turn red; this will limit pest damage from fruitworms and stinkbugs. Keep tomatoes on the kitchen counter to ripen completely.

Common Problem

If you notice large sections of leaves missing from the plant, look for a 3- to 4-inch green worm with a horn on its rear. Tomato hornworms are surprisingly difficult to spot. For severe infestations where handpicking cannot control them, apply *Bacillus thuringiensis* every 7 days.

CHAPTER EIGHT

Alliums and Herbs

Garlic
Onions
Basil
Cilantro
Mint
Parsley
Rosemary
Sage
Thyme

Garlic

Family: Amaryllidaceae

Growing zones: N/A

Growing season(s): cool weather

Spacing: 6 to 8 inches

Start indoors or direct sow: direct sow

Indoor sowing date: N/A

Earliest outdoor planting: 2 weeks before average first frost

Soil temperature: N/A

Fall planting: N/A

Sun needs: 6+ hours

Water needs: low

Harvest category: one harvest

Suggested varieties for beginners: softneck for warmer regions, hardneck for cooler regions

Keep in Mind Tip: Although it's possible to plant garlic cloves you buy at the grocery store, I don't recommend it. First, this garlic is usually not certified disease-free, so you risk contaminating your garden soil for years to come. Second, you don't know whether that variety will grow in your region. Most garlic in grocery stores is softneck garlic, which grows well in the South but doesn't tolerate cold as well as hardneck types.

Snapshot

Garlic is one of the easiest crops for a home gardener to grow. Planted in the fall for the following season, garlic requires little maintenance and is one of the first plants to begin growing in the early spring. An adaptable crop, garlic can be grown in the ground, in raised beds, and in containers.

Starting

Purchase certified disease-free bulbs of garlic from a reputable seed supplier. At around the time of your first fall frost, separate individual cloves from the bulb and plant pointy-side up in 2-inch-deep trenches. Cover with soil, and in cold-climate areas, spread an additional 1 to 2 inches of mulch. Water well at planting.

Growing

Garlic will likely sprout in the fall, stop growing through the winter, and start growing again in the late winter. Water isn't necessary during this dormant period; begin consistent light irrigation in the spring if rainfall is scarce. Keep the area well weeded (mulch helps).

Harvesting and Storing

Southern gardeners may start harvesting garlic in mid-May; northern growers may not harvest until late July. In either case, watch for the lower half of the leaves to turn brown and die off. Use a trowel to dig around the bulb to loosen the soil. Pull out the bulbs and move them to a shaded, well-ventilated location (such as a garage). Lay the bulbs in single layers or hang them. Set a fan on them if you live in a humid location and let them "cure" for 2 to 4 weeks. Curing is complete when the necks of the bulbs completely dry out. Clip the bulbs from the dry foliage, trim the roots, and move them to a root cellar or pantry for storage. Save the biggest bulbs in a loosely closed brown paper bag for your next crop.

Common Problem

Garlic usually has few problems. Abnormally rainy springs can cause poor bulb development, as can planting the cloves too close together. If you live in a wet area, plant garlic in raised beds or containers.

Onions

~~~~~~
CONTAINER-FRIENDLY, RAISED BED–FRIENDLY
~~~~~~

Family: Amaryllidaceae

Growing zones: N/A

Growing season(s): cool weather

Spacing: 6 inches

Start indoors or direct sow: start indoors or purchase transplants or sets

Indoor sowing date: 10 weeks before transplant (16 weeks before average last frost)

Earliest outdoor planting: 6 weeks before average last frost

Soil temperature: 50° to 95°

Fall planting: N/A

Sun needs: 6+ hours

Water needs: moderate

Harvest category: one harvest

Suggested varieties for beginners: Ailsa Craig (long-day), Yellow Granex (short-day)

Keep in Mind Tip: If you want to eat "green onions" (scallions), you can harvest the leaves at any time. Just keep in mind that those leaves help nourish the developing bulb; the more leaves you remove, the smaller the bulb will be. Consider planting a crop just for scallions that you can harvest throughout the season.

Snapshot

Onions are one of the most commonly used vegetables for cooking. The key to growing good onions is to choose the correct seeds, sets, or transplants for your area. In order to harvest a large bulb, gardeners in the southern United States must grow short-day onions, and gardeners in the North must grow long-day ones. Gardeners in the middle parts of the country can try either type or purchase "day-neutral" varieties.

Starting

Most beginning gardeners plant onions from transplants or sets. Transplants look like scallions from the grocery store; sets look like baby onion bulbs. Most sets are long-day onions, so if you live in the South, double-check the variety or your onions won't bulb. Plant onions in well-drained soil amended with plenty of organic matter. Transplants should be planted with the white part underground; bury sets just beneath the soil's surface.

Growing

Keep the area well weeded. In the early months of growth, rainfall will likely provide sufficient water, but during hotter times of year or periods of drought, ensure onions receive 1 to 2 inches of irrigation per week. After the soil has warmed, apply a layer of mulch to help with weed control and to conserve moisture.

Harvesting and Storing

Onions are ready to harvest when the tops have yellowed and fallen over. Dig out the bulbs, being careful not to stab them with the trowel. Transfer them to a shaded, well-ventilated location where you can lay them in single layers or hang them. Let them "cure" until the stems have dried out and no moisture remains in the stem when you clip off the foliage. Store in a cool area such as a root cellar or the bottom of your pantry.

Common Problem

If the onion plant sends out a tall flower stalk before it's ready to harvest, the plant has bolted and bulb production has stopped. Early bolting is typically caused by environmental stress such as extreme temperature fluctuations or water issues. Keep the area mulched to moderate soil temperature. Upon bolting, harvest the onion bulbs and use them before other onions, because they will not store well.

Basil

Family: Lamiaceae

Growing zones: N/A

Growing season(s): warm weather

Spacing: 12 inches

Start indoors or direct sow: either, or purchase transplants

Indoor sowing date: 4 weeks before average last frost

Earliest outdoor planting: after last spring frost

Soil temperature: 60° to 90°

Fall planting: N/A

Sun needs: 6+ hours

Water needs: moderate

Harvest category: all season

Suggested varieties for beginners: sweet basil, cinnamon basil, Genovese

Preparation Tip: Turn extra basil into a simple pesto. Combine 20 to 30 basil leaves, ¼ cup of olive oil, 2 garlic cloves, ½ teaspoon of salt, ¼ teaspoon of pepper, 1 table-spoon of pine nuts, and 2 tablespoons of Parmesan cheese in a food processor or blender and blend to a paste. Serve over angel-hair pasta or make larger batches to freeze.

Snapshot

Possibly the most popular herb in the home garden, basil is beloved for its fragrant and tasty leaves. Enjoyed fresh in Italian dishes or made into basil pesto, no home garden should be without this summer delight.

Starting

Basil thrives in warm weather. It will die in a frost and suffer damage when nights dip below 50°. For this reason, wait to plant basil (seeds or transplants) until a week or more after your last frost. If direct sowing, scatter seeds on top of the soil and scrape them in with your fingers. Water well and keep moist until germination.

Growing

Keep basil consistently moist but not waterlogged. For an all-season harvest, keep the plant trimmed, starting at about 6 inches high so it will bush out. Trim the tips of the stems when the leaves start forming a tight cluster in the center. Without proper pruning, those clusters will bloom into flowers (and eventually seeds), and the quality of the remaining leaves will decline.

Harvesting and Storing

Harvest basil early and often, and use fresh leaves immediately. If you need to store the leaves, cut them with stems that are long enough to place upright in a glass of water in the refrigerator.

Common Problem

Basil loves to flower and go to seed quickly. But pollinators and beneficial insects love those flowers. Get the best of both worlds by planting multiple plants, keeping one trimmed for fresh use and letting the others flower. When the flower pods dry out, gather the seeds to save for next season.

Cilantro

Family: Apiaceae

Growing zones: N/A

Growing season(s): cool weather

Spacing: 6 inches

Start indoors or direct sow: direct sow

Indoor sowing date: N/A

Earliest outdoor planting: as soon as soil can be worked

Soil temperature: 55° to 68°

Fall planting: 4 to 6 weeks before average first frost

Sun needs: 6+ hours

Water needs: moderate

Harvest category: weather dependent

Suggested varieties for beginners: Slo-bolt, Santo

Fun Fact: Does cilantro taste like soap to you? It's not just you. A certain percentage of the population has a genetic sensitivity to aldehydes in cilantro leaves, which makes them perceive the flavor as soapy.

Snapshot

A love-it-or-hate-it herb, cilantro is a staple in many gardens. Cilantro, unlike the foods it's usually paired with, hates hot weather and prefers the cool temperatures of fall, winter, and spring.

Starting

Sow cilantro seeds directly into the garden about 2 inches apart, thinning to 6 inches apart. Cilantro likes well-drained soil enriched with compost. Plant several plants if you plan to freeze or preserve it.

Growing

If you live in a hotter climate, mulch the plants well and consider afternoon shade to keep soil temperatures as low as possible for as long as possible.

Harvesting and Storing

Start harvesting cilantro when it's 6 inches tall. When the plant starts to bolt and flower, leave it, and you can harvest the seeds as the spice coriander.

Common Problem

Cilantro bolts quickly in warm weather, so harvest it frequently while it's small. The leaves turn bitter when they become feathery and the center stalk starts growing tall. Sow succession plantings to keep a continuous supply, then let the bolted plants flower and go to seed. As the plants drop the seed they may continuously self-sow. If you grow cilantro in the fall, you may have a longer harvest window.

Mint

Family: Lamiaceae

Growing zones: N/A

Growing season(s): perennial in zones 3 (some varieties) +

Spacing: 12 to 18 inches

Start indoors or direct sow: purchase transplants

Indoor sowing date: N/A

Earliest outdoor planting: early spring

Soil temperature: N/A

Fall planting: N/A

Sun needs: 6+ hours

Water needs: high

Harvest category: all season

Suggested varieties for beginners: peppermint, spearmint, chocolate mint, lemon balm

Fun Fact: Peppermint is a well-known tummy soother. Pinch off fresh leaves and steep them in hot water for 10 minutes. Add honey if desired. (Not recommended for young children.)

Snapshot

Mints of all kinds are a delight in the garden. Just make sure to plant them in a well-contained place, as the plants spread invasively. Containers are the best solution. Use mint in hot tea, summertime fruit salads, and in cold, refreshing mint water. Once you learn the variety of uses for homegrown mint, you'll be glad you added it to your garden.

Starting

Purchase potted mint from your local garden center and plant it in rich, moist soil. It requires more water than other herbs, so consider this when combining herbs in large pots or beds.

Growing

Besides keeping mint plants well watered (especially during the heat of the summer), the best care you can provide is pruning. Cut the plants frequently to keep them producing tender new leaves.

Harvesting and Storing

Cut mint as needed for fresh use. If it becomes woody, cut back the entire plant to promote new growth (you can do this a few times throughout the season). Dry the cuttings in a dehydrator or hang them upside down in a dark, airy location. Strip the leaves and store them in clean jars.

Common Problem

If your mint plant stops growing and seems to show woody rather than tender growth, most likely it has outgrown its pot. Wait for mild weather (not high heat or winter cold) and take the entire plant out of the pot. Divide it with a sharp knife and replant one division in fresh soil. Plant the other division in a separate container (or give to a friend). Water it well.

Parsley

Family: Apiaceae

Growing zones: N/A

Growing season(s): cool-weather biennial

Spacing: 10 inches

Start indoors or direct sow: either, or purchase transplants

Indoor sowing date: 4 weeks before transplant (6 weeks before average last frost)

Earliest outdoor planting: 2 weeks before average last frost

Soil temperature: 50° to 80°

Fall planting: in the South, plant transplants 4 weeks before first frost

Sun needs: 4+ hours

Water needs: moderate

Harvest category: all season, weather dependent in some areas

Suggested varieties for beginners: Italian dark green, curly parsley

Fun Fact: Whether parsley bolts in the first year or completes its growing cycle in the second year, if left to flower and drop seed, it may self-sow, giving you a continuous supply.

Snapshot

Parsley is said to intensify other flavors. When you grow it yourself, the flavor profile amplifies. Dried parsley and store-bought parsley simply do not compare to the homegrown herb. When parsley is established and grown under ideal conditions, you can expect to harvest it for well over a year, until its growth cycle causes it to flower and set seed in its second year.

Starting

Though you can sow parsley from seed, it can take a long time to germinate. Many first-time gardeners prefer to purchase transplants. Plant parsley in moist but well-drained soil with plenty of organic matter.

Growing

Keep plants evenly watered. In the hotter summers of the South, parsley benefits from afternoon shade, because high temperatures and water stress can cause it to bolt in the first year. Southern growers may find a fall planting to be more successful and will be able to harvest leaves all winter.

Harvesting and Storing

Begin harvesting when the plant reaches 6 inches in height, and harvest as needed. Or, for a larger harvest for drying, cut the plant back to 1 to 2 inches above soil level, where it will regrow leaves. Parsley can be dried, but the flavor will weaken considerably.

Common Problem

When the plant produces a tall center stalk, it has bolted. The leaves can still be used, though the flavor might become bitter. To prevent parsley from bolting, mulch the plants well and keep them watered to limit stress, especially in the hot summer.

Rosemary

Family: Lamiaceae

Growing zones: N/A

Growing season(s): perennial in zones 7+

Spacing: 36 inches

Start indoors or direct sow: purchase transplants

Indoor sowing date: N/A

Earliest outdoor planting: early spring

Soil temperature: N/A

Fall planting: N/A

Sun needs: 4+ hours

Water needs: low

Harvest category: all season (zones 7+), weather dependent (zones 6-)

Suggested varieties for beginners: N/A

Troubleshooting Tip: Rosemary may not survive outdoors where temperatures dip below 5°; gardeners in borderline zones may have success planting rosemary in a southern-exposure location or in the ground with heavy mulch. Northern gardeners can bring rosemary pots inside for the winter.

Snapshot

A beautifully fragrant shrub, rosemary is perfect for a container patio garden and mixes well with other herbs. Light, well-drained soil is best for the plant, and it tolerates drought. After a few years, rosemary will become tough and woody; plan to replace old plants every few years for the best-quality herb.

Starting

Purchase a potted transplant from a local garden center. Water it well at transplant and it shouldn't have any trouble getting established.

Growing

Rosemary grown in the ground rarely requires supplemental irrigation. Potted rosemary should be monitored occasionally to ensure the soil doesn't dry out completely.

Harvesting and Storing

Snip leaves as necessary for fresh use. To harvest for storage purposes, cut the stems a few inches above where they have become woody, but don't harvest more than one-third of the plant at a time. Hang the cuttings upside down in a dark, airy location. When they're dry, strip the leaves and store them in a clean jar.

Common Problem

If the leaves turn brown, the plant likely received too much water. To avoid this problem, cut down on watering or, if the plant is outside, move it to a sheltered location during rainy periods or mulch it to help moderate the moisture.

Sage

Family: Lamiaceae

Growing zones: N/A

Growing season(s): perennial in zones 4 to 8

Spacing: 18 inches

Start indoors or direct sow: purchase transplants

Indoor sowing date: N/A

Earliest outdoor planting: early spring

Soil temperature: N/A

Fall planting: N/A

Sun needs: 6+ hours

Water needs: low

Harvest category: all season

Suggested varieties for beginners: culinary sage

Fun Fact: Sage can be grown indoors on a sunny windowsill, giving you a fresh supply of the herb all winter. Choose a compact variety and cut back any flowers that form.

Snapshot

Sage is most commonly known as the spice in Thanksgiving dressing, but it's also a staple in sausage, meatloaf, and pork dishes. In most zones, sage grows as a perennial. It may lose its leaves in the winter but will regrow in the spring. In areas that don't receive frost, sage may not grow year-round because of a lack of chilling time needed for new growth.

Starting

Purchase a potted sage plant at your local garden center and plant it in light, well-drained soil. Water it well at planting.

Growing

Sage prefers full sun, but it may need partial shade in areas with hot summers. After the first year, cut back the entire plant to half its size after new growth begins to appear. This will keep the plant in check and also encourage new tender growth.

Harvesting and Storing

Pick sage leaves as needed for fresh use. Sage leaves can also be dried when cut back the second year and ground into spice.

Common Problem

Once established, sage prefers not to have a lot of water. If the soil is too heavy and rainfall causes it to stay saturated, it can show signs of disease. If you have heavier soil, add sand or perlite to help with drainage.

Thyme

Family: Lamiaceae

Growing zones: N/A

Growing season(s): perennial in zones 4+

Spacing: 12 inches

Start indoors or direct sow: purchase transplants

Indoor sowing date: N/A

Earliest outdoor planting: early spring

Soil temperature: N/A

Fall planting: N/A

Sun needs: 4+ hours

Water needs: low

Harvest category: all season

Suggested varieties for beginners: common thyme, English thyme, creeping thyme

Keep in Mind Tip: Because thyme will make its home in most gardens for several years, choose its location carefully.

Snapshot

A fuss-free, low-growing herb, thyme can grow in a trailing fashion or like a shrub. In zones 4 and above, thyme is a hardy perennial, and you can harvest from an established plant year-round.

Starting

Purchase potted thyme from your local nursery. Plant in well-draining soil; a container is a perfect choice.

Growing

Besides the initial watering, thyme requires little extra care. If you live in zone 4, mulch the plants before winter to protect them from the cold. Thyme doesn't like too much moisture, so mulch with fine gravel or pine needles instead of wood mulch.

Harvesting and Storing

Thyme can be harvested for fresh eating year-round for most gardeners. But if you want to dry larger quantities, cut back the entire plant just before it flowers, leaving 3 to 4 inches of growth at the bottom. The plant will regrow. Hang the sprigs upside down in a dark but ventilated room. Strip the leaves when they are dry and place them in a clean jar for storage.

Common Problem

After a few years, a thyme plant will become woody and the quality of the leaves will decline. Plan to replace your thyme plant every few years for a steady supply of high-quality, fragrant leaves.

Zone Map

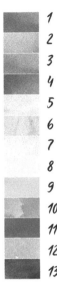

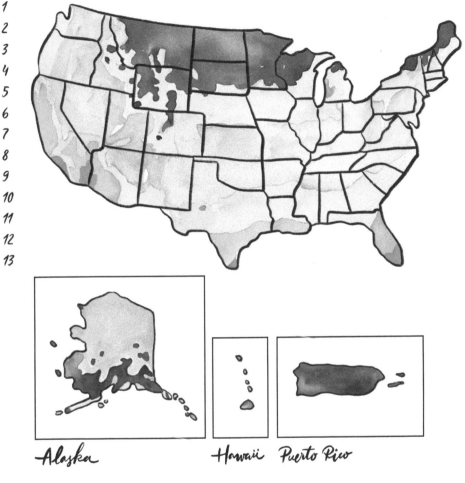

Alaska Hawaii Puerto Rico

Resources

Find your average frost date

The Old Farmer's Almanac, https://www.almanac.com/gardening/frostdates

Find your local cooperative extension service by zip code

Gardening Know How, https://www.gardeningknowhow.com/extension-search

Find soil-testing labs by state

Gardening Products Review, https://gardeningproductsreview.com/state
-by-state-list-soil-testing-labs-cooperative-extension-offices

Garden tools

Gardener's Supply Company, https://www.gardeners.com

Seed and plant suppliers

Baker Creek Heirloom Seeds, https://www.rareseeds.com

Seed Savers Exchange, https://www.seedsavers.org

Southern Exposure Seed Exchange, https://southernexposure.com

Territorial Seed Company, https://territorialseed.com

References

Bradley, Fern Marshall, Barbara W. Ellis, and Deborah Martin. *The Organic Gardener's Handbook of Natural Pest and Disease Control*. New York: Rodale, Inc., 2009.

Bradley, Fern Marshall, Barbara W. Ellis, and Ellen Phillips. *Rodale's Ultimate Encyclopedia of Organic Gardening*. New York: Rodale, Inc., 2009.

Bradley, Fern Marshall, and Jane Courtier. *Vegetable Gardening*. White Plains, NY: Toucan Books, 2006.

Cool Springs Press. *Gardening Complete*. Minneapolis: Cool Springs Press, 2018.

Damrosch, Barbara. *The Garden Primer*. New York: Workman Publishing, Inc., 2008.

Harrington, J. F. "Soil Temperature Conditions for Vegetable Seed Germination." University of California at Davis. Accessed October 18, 2019. https://extension .oregonstate.edu/sites/default/files/documents/12281/soiltemps.pdf.

McCrate, Colin, and Brad Halm. *High-Yield Vegetable Gardening*. North Adams, MA: Storey Publishing, 2015.

Reich, Lee. *Weedless Gardening*. New York: Workman Publishing Co., Inc., 2001.

Southern Exposure Seed Exchange (blog). "The Major Plant Families in a Vegetable Garden." Accessed October 22, 2019. http://www.southernexposure.com /the-major-plant-families-in-a-vegetable-garden-ezp-190.html.

Index

Acknowledgments

To my husband, Matt. You've never wavered in supporting me, from building garden trellises and fences to encouraging me to write this book. Your tireless work to support our family has enabled me to live my dream.

To Drew and Alyssa, some of my favorite memories with you include enjoying the garden together. To Dad, for always believing in me and supporting me in everything I've set out to do. To Beverly, Glenn, Anita, Amber, and Zac, for your unending encouragement and support.

To Teresa, for diligently praying for me through these writing deadlines. To Tiffany, Rachel, Wendi, and Shy, for checking in with me and praying for me. To Megan, for picking up extra podcast and blog work so I could focus on this book.

To Kent, for taking a chance on listening to this new girl's podcast in its early days. You could run circles around me with your knowledge; thank you for sharing it so freely. Your friendship across the miles has been a sweet blessing.

To Mr. Atchley, my high school English teacher. I thought you were crazy when you told me I'd be a writer someday. You'll be proud to know I used your pre-writing techniques for this book.

To my virtual gardening mentors Melissa K. Norris and Joe Lamp'l. You've been so generous not only to teach the masses about gardening but also to support and encourage me as I seek to do the same in my own little corner of the world.

To the publishing team at Callisto for your work behind the scenes. Thank you, Matt, for seeing something in me that I didn't. Thank you, Ada and Claire, for being such a joy to work with and for encouraging me as I endeavored to bring your vision for this work to life.

Finally, to my first love, Jesus. You are full of abundant gifts; thank you for giving me the garden and meeting me there.

About the Author

Jill McSheehy teaches thousands of beginning gardeners how to grow their own vegetables, fruit, and herbs through her podcast, *The Beginner's Garden Podcast*, and on her website, journeywithjill.net. A self-taught gardener, Jill's background is not in horticulture. After earning a bachelor's degree from Arkansas Tech University, she spent a decade as business development manager at a local Ford dealership. Jill didn't begin her first garden until 2013 after she became a stay-at-home mom. But she grew to love her newfound passion and wanted to pass it on to other aspiring gardeners. Jill, her husband, Matt, and their two children, Drew and Alyssa, live on three acres in the Russellville, Arkansas, area. When not tending to her 2,500-square-foot garden and flock of chickens, Jill enjoys reading, camping with her family, and canning vegetables and fruit from her garden.

CPSIA information can be obtained
at www.ICGtesting.com
Printed in the USA
LVHW020932190323
741869LV00002B/3